75 QUESTIONS & ANSWERS about PREPARING for the TEMPLE

"Brother Gaskill's careful approach to the questions addressed in this book will equip parents, grandparents, and Church leaders to help those they love to have more meaningful experiences in the temple. There are principles in this book that will help the newest deacon or Beehive have a more powerful experience as they participate in baptisms for the dead, and there are principles that will touch the heart and expand the mind of the most seasoned temple worker. *This book is for everyone!*"

—G. Shad Martin, director of preservice training, Brigham Young University

"For members of The Church of Jesus Christ of Latter-day Saints, making and keeping temple covenants is critical for their exaltation and eternal life. Dr. Gaskill does a commendable job asking and answering essential questions for those who are planning to attend the temple—especially for those attending the temple for the first time."

—David K. Fossum, counselor in the St. Paul Temple Presidency, 2010–2013

"Alonzo Gaskill has created a most welcome and needed book for your preparation to attend the temple. He has skillfully addressed questions that are on the minds of all who are preparing to enter the Lord's holy house. This book not only covers questions you might have about preparing for the temple, but it also lets you know what you can expect once you enter the temple.

"Being ready to attend the temple is *your* sacred responsibility, and this book will be a wonderful asset in your preparations. It contains vital information for everyone who is planning to receive their temple endowment or the sealing ordinances. And it is a great review for lifetime members as they seek to understand and appreciate the doctrines, ordinances, and covenants received in the house of the Lord.

"This book will help relieve the anxiety and stress associated with the initial experience of attending the temple; and it will bless your life by helping you to have a glorious experience in the house of the Lord. It is the perfect book to assist you in your preparation to enter the Lord's holy house."

—Ed J. Pinegar, former Manti Temple President (2009–2012) and author of *The Temple: Gaining Knowledge and Power in the House of the Lord*

"*75 Questions and Answers about Preparing for the Temple* should be required reading for everyone preparing to receive their endowment. Dr. Gaskill's answers to these tough questions can put every member at ease and allow them to feel the Spirit and be prepared their first experience in the temple. Even if you have already attended the temple for years, *you need this book.* I'm serious, buy this book and read it with your children, your quorum, your missionary, and your friends. You'll be grateful that you did."

—Hank Smith, assistant teaching professor of ancient scripture, Brigham Young University

75 QUESTIONS & ANSWERS

about PREPARING for the

TEMPLE

ALONZO L. GASKILL

CFI

An imprint of Cedar Fort, Inc.
Springville, Utah

ISBN 13: 978-1-4621-2334-6

Published by CFI, an imprint of Cedar Fort, Inc.
2373 W. 700 S., Springville, UT 84663
Distributed by Cedar Fort, Inc., www.cedarfort.com

LIBRARY OF CONGRESS CATALOGING-IN-PUBLICATION DATA

Names: Gaskill, Alonzo L., author.
Title: 75 questions and answers about preparing for the temple / Alonzo L. Gaskill.
Other titles: Seventy-five questions and answers about preparing for the temple
Description: Springville, Utah : CFI, an imprint of Cedar Fort, Inc., [2019] | Includes bibliographical references and index.
Identifiers: LCCN 2018053786 (print) | LCCN 2018060747 (ebook) | ISBN 9781462130078 (epub, pdf, mobi) | ISBN 9781462123346 (perfect bound : alk. paper)
Subjects: LCSH: Mormon temples--Miscellanea. | Temple endowments (Mormon Church)--Miscellanea. | Temple work (Mormon Church)--Miscellanea. | Church of Jesus Christ of Latter-day Saints--Doctrines--Miscellanea. | Mormon Church--Doctrines--Miscellanea.
Classification: LCC BX8643.T4 (ebook) | LCC BX8643.T4 G367 2019 (print) | DDC 264/.09332--dc23
LC record available at https://lccn.loc.gov/2018053786

Cover design by Wes Wheeler
Cover design © 2019 Cedar Fort, Inc.
Edited by Melissa Caldwell, Justin Greer, and Nicole Terry
Typeset by Kaitlin Barwick

Printed in the United States of America

10 9 8 7 6 5 4 3 2 1

Printed on acid-free paper

For Lisa Spice, who expressed the need for such a book
and who repeatedly encouraged me to write it.

Also by

Alonzo L. Gaskill

Converted: True Mormon Conversion Stories from 15 Religions

Know Your Religions, Volume 3: A Comparative Look
at Mormonism and Jehovah's Witnesses

Temple Reflections: Insights into the House of the Lord

Catholic and Mormon: A Theological Conversion

Miracles of the Book of Mormon:
A Guide to the Symbolic Messages

Miracles of the New Testament:
A Guide to the Symbolic Messages

Miracles of the Old Testament:
A Guide to the Symbolic Messages

Remember: Sacred Truths We Must Never Forget

The Lost Teachings of Jesus on the Sacred Place of Women

Love at Home: Insights from the Lives of Latter-day Prophets

The Truth about Eden: Understanding the Fall
and Our Temple Experience

Odds Are You're Going to Be Exalted:
Evidence that the Plan of Salvation Works!

The Nativity: Rediscover the Most Important Birth in All History

The Savior and the Serpent: Unlocking the Doctrine of the Fall

The Lost Language of Symbolism: An Essential Guide for
Recognizing and Interpreting Symbols of the Gospel

Our Savior's Love: Hope & Healing in Christ

Sacred Symbols: Finding Meaning in Rites,
Rituals, and Ordinances

65 Questions and Answers about Patriarchal Blessings

Contents

What to Do Once You've Received Your Temple Ordinances

Acknowledgments

Novelist John Green famously noted, "In the end, what makes a book valuable is not the paper it's printed on, but the thousands of hours of work by dozens of people who are dedicated to creating the best possible reading experience for you." And so it is! Thus, I express my sincere appreciation to the many formative reviewers who read my manuscript during its developmental stage and offered suggestions to improve what I had written. I am indebted to each of the following individuals: David A. Butler, Melissa Caldwell, Matthew B. Christensen, Paul E. Damron, Dr. Guy L. Dorius, Lori K. Gaskill, John Harrison, Hannah L. Jorgensen, Dr. Rick B. Jorgensen, G. Shad Martin, Elder Khumbulani Mdletshe of the Seventy, Lani Moore, Dr. Richard G. Moore, Dr. Ed J. Pinegar, Denney E. Pugmire, Wayne G. Pullan, Andy H. Skelton, Lisa L. Spice, Dr. Anthony R. Sweat, and Nicole Terry. To each I offer my heartfelt thanks and acknowledge my indebtedness.

In addition, I express appreciation to the handful of summative reviewers who read the completed manuscript and offered their suggestions and encouragement.

I also express my earnest gratitude to the hundreds of friends and acquaintances who submitted their questions during the formative stage of writing this book. Without their suggestions and questions, I believe this book would have failed to answer many questions commonly held by individuals who are preparing to attend the temple for the first time or who have just gone to the temple for their first time.

I express my thanks to Greta Motiejunaite Soha and Seth Soha for the beautiful image of the clasped hands (from the face of the Salt Lake Temple), which appears in Question #51 of this book and which they have graciously allowed me to use in this publication.

I should point out what Dr. Seuss once said:

> So the writer who breeds
> more words than he needs
> is making a chore
> for the reader who reads.

I must admit, I am often guilty of transgressing this rule of good writing. Consequently, I express my indebtedness to Jan Nyholm, my formative editor. Jan, thanks for working your magic over the years, always helping me to be more succinct in what I have said. I am so grateful for the service you have rendered. You are a generous soul.

Finally, I remind the reader that this book is not an official publication of The Church of Jesus Christ of Latter-day Saints nor of my employer, Brigham Young University.

Introduction

O ne of the most unique aspects of The Church of Jesus Christ of Latter-day Saints is its use of temples as a form of worship and as a means of uniting families and connecting individuals to God for time and for all eternity. No other major Christian denomination has temple worship and temple ordinances as part of its faith. Unquestionably, Latter-day Saints are most fortunate to have access to these revealed ordinances and to have access to the power and knowledge available to those who worthily and regularly attend the temples that literally dot the earth.

For me personally, attending the temple has been a wonderful and enriching experience. Quite literally, each of the ordinances has significant meaning *in* and application *to* my life, and I continue to find myself intrigued by all that the Spirit teaches me as I regularly attend the house of the Lord.

However, too many Latter-day Saints go to the temple for the first time unprepared for the experience. President Ezra Taft Benson (1899–1994), thirteenth President of the Church, expressed his concern about how poorly we prepare the youth for their temple experience:

> The temple is a sacred place, and the ordinances in the temple are of a sacred character. Because of its sacredness we are sometimes reluctant to say *anything* about the temple to our children and grandchildren. As a consequence, many do not develop a real desire to go to the temple, or when they go there, they do so without much background to prepare them for the obligations and covenants they enter into.
>
> I believe a proper understanding or background will immeasurably help prepare our youth for the temple.[1]

Similarly, President Boyd K. Packer (1924–2015), former President of the Quorum of the Twelve Apostles, wrote, "Members of the Church are not willing to talk about [temple] matters . . . Lacking knowledge, some [who have not been through the temple] develop strange explanations about the work of our temples."[2] In 1971, the First Presidency of the Church sent out a circular letter stating, "It has come to our attention that many of those planning to go to the temple for the first time are not properly oriented as to what to expect there. Under such circumstances they may fail to receive adequate understanding from their experience in the temple."[3] A lack of preparation certainly increases the likelihood that those attending for the first time will not have the positive experience the temple is intended to provide. As an example, I knew two young men who were best friends and who received their endowment on the same day, in the same temple. One of the two had a wonderful, uplifting experience and seemed well prepared for what he encountered during his endowment. His best friend, however, was not as well prepared and, in many ways, found his first experience in the temple less than uplifting, somewhat confusing, and not the spiritual experience he was expecting. During their endowment, these two young men were taught the exact same things in the exact same ways but had two very different experiences—largely because of how prepared (or unprepared) they were.

In part, proper preparation is the responsibility of the individual who is seeking to participate in the ordinances of the temple. However, those who have not yet attended the temple often don't know where to start in their personal preparation. Consequently, those of us who have already participated in baptisms for the dead, the temple's initiatory and endowment ordinances, or a sealing ceremony have a responsibility to make sure that those who know nothing of the details of these sacred rites and ordinances are sufficiently prepared for what they are going to experience, so that they will have a positive experience when they go to the temple.

Elder Khumbulani Mdletshe (b. 1964), of the Seventy, suggested that going to the temple for the first time should carry the anticipation and surprise a young child might feel at Christmastime. When we go to the temple for the first time, we should understand that God has a great gift for us—a gift we are about to receive. Just as little children are traditionally *thrilled* by the gifts given on Christmas, members of the Church *should* find their experience in the temple even more satisfying than the largely material gifts on that holiday.[4] However, for some, this is not their experience—mostly, as President Benson suggested, because of their lack of preparation. A friend of mine shared an analogy that he uses to describe how many members approach temple preparation. It goes as follows:

> Imagine you live in a culture in which children are told how wonderful oranges are. Throughout their entire lives they hear about how awesome and delicious the fruit is, but the children are always forbidden to partake of oranges—because their palates are not yet mature enough to appreciate this wonderful fruit. Indeed, they are not even allowed to see an orange, let alone watch an adult partake of one. Nevertheless, they are told time and again that *eventually* the day will come when they too will be permitted to taste of oranges, and they are excitedly informed that they will absolutely love *everything* about them.
>
> *Finally*, the time arrives. The young man (or woman) is now older, and it is determined that he is ready to partake of the beloved orange. On the appointed day, this budding young adult is placed alone in a room with a singular orange. It is perfect and plump, ready to be eaten. However, the young man is given no instructions as to how to eat the orange. He has no experience eating them and has never seen another person eat one. With slight anxiety, the youth picks the orange up, sniffs it, and then—not knowing the orange needs to be peeled—takes a small bite of it. It is remarkably bitter to the taste, and the experience is shocking. Our friend feels like he has been deceived by the many adults who spoke of how *absolutely wonderful* oranges are. The young adult determines that he hates oranges and, frankly, distrusts those who misled him about how supposedly wonderful they are.

Had this young person been given some instructions about how to eat an orange, he most likely would have had a pleasant experience, but the lack of knowledge—and lack of preparation for the experience—left him terribly disappointed, surprised, and a bit jaded.

In some ways, this is how some of us approach temple preparation for our children, grandchildren, and friends. We tell them over and over again how great the temple is going to be for them—and we gush over how they are going to just love *everything* about it—but then we do such a poor job preparing them for it that some end up having needlessly negative experiences their first time attending, as they aren't really sure what to do with the things they learn and experience in the temple.

This isn't to suggest that there is a singular way to enjoy the temple any more than there is only one way to peel or eat an orange. Just as an orange can be peeled by hand, cut into wedges, turned into juice, and so on, so also there are many approaches to understanding and enjoying the temple. Yet, in both cases, we must instruct those preparing to partake. If we do so, we increase the likelihood that they will have a good experience—and that they will understand that in order to fully enjoy what they are about to receive, they must peel back the skin and really sink their teeth *per se* into the meat of the orange or ordinance. If we do not properly prepare them, they may just be left with the bitter taste of the outer peel—which is not truly what the endowment or the orange is about.

If, because of the newness of the experience, those we love have a bad experience their first time in the temple, it may be partially *our* fault. In addition, if their first experience is poor, they may not want to return. We really *must* do a better job of preparing those whom we love to have a sweet and wonderful experience in the temple. We can do that if we will give them a bit of clear instruction and help establish clear expectations.[5]

Just as the orange, if eaten properly, is sweet and delicious to the taste, one's first encounter with the ordinances of the temple can be delightful. However, if one is unprepared, his or her temple

4

experience may be different than expected and, thus, confusing or disappointing. As we will address in this book, symbolic clothing, gestures, stories, architecture, and even policies can sometimes surprise and confuse patrons. If they are properly prepared to expect and understand these symbolic elements of the temple—and if they are more aware of the policies and practices associated with temple worship—they are more likely to have a positive, Spirit-filled experience. Families and friends really should be more proactive in preparing those who are about to enter the temple.

It is for this purpose that this book has been written. Each of the questions addressed herein was actually posed to me by members who were about to attend the temple for the first time or who had recently gone through the temple for their first time and wished that they had been more prepared. While I have carefully avoided discussing in detail those things we make a covenant not to reveal—and I have been cautious to stay within the bounds set within the temple itself—nevertheless, I have tried to speak candidly and informatively about what one will experience in the house of the Lord.[6] It is my earnest hope that all who enter the holy temple will find meaning and beauty in what they experience and be sufficiently prepared so that they can strongly feel the Spirit of the Lord therein.

Notes

1. Ezra Taft Benson, *The Teachings of Ezra Taft Benson* (Salt Lake City, UT: Bookcraft, 1998), 251–52, emphasis added.
2. Boyd K. Packer, *The Holy Temple* (Salt Lake City, UT: Bookcraft, 1980), 30.
3. "So You Are Going to the Temple," Joseph Fieldling Smith, Harold B. Lee, and N. Eldon Tanner, circular letter, February 12, 1971, 1.
4. Elder Khumbulani Mdletshe, personal correspondence, June 11, 2018.
5. My summary of personal correspondence from John Harrison, May 1, 2018.
6. Ed J. Pinegar recently wrote, "As the *Encyclopedia of Mormonism* remarks, members of the Church can discuss everything about the temple except [the] specific details regarding the temple ceremonies—the signs and tokens and the specific language of the ceremony and covenants." Ed J. Pinegar, *The Temple: Gaining Knowledge and Power in the House of the Lord* (American Fork, UT: Covenant Communications, 2014), 198.

The Doctrine of Temple Work

1

What is the purpose of temples?

The ultimate purpose of temples is the exaltation of families. President Russell M. Nelson (b. 1924), seventeenth President of the Church, has noted, "This Church was restored so that families could be formed, sealed, and exalted eternally. . . . All church activities, advancements, quorums, and classes are means to the end of an exalted family." President Nelson added, "While salvation is an individual matter, exaltation is a family matter."[1] President Ezra Taft Benson (1899–1994), thirteenth President of the Church, similarly taught, "The temple is an ever-present reminder that God intends the family to be eternal."[2] We need our families if we hope to dwell with God for eternity. The temple really is the place where eternal families begin, and it is a place that helps us to feel deeply connected to both our ancestors and our posterity.

Another purpose of temples is to allow the faithful to enter into covenants with their God—covenants that, if kept, will both protect us from the influence of the adversary and exalt us in the kingdom of our God. Rich blessings are promised to those who worthily enter into and keep sacred covenants. The temple is the one place upon the face of this Earth where certain covenants can be received. If you wish to have *more* of the Spirit in your life and *less* of the influence of the adversary, the temple is the perfect retreat. Temples are places we go to if we want to get *away from* the world so that we can more easily *make contact* with God. Because the distractions of this fallen world (e.g., cell phones, computers, entertainment, work, money, worldly apparel, etc.) are not permitted in the temple, there one can more readily focus on the things that matter most—and thereby more easily make contact with one's creator. Thus, the Lord has called His holy house "a house of prayer" (D&C 88:119).

Temples also function as a set-apart site wherein we can redeem our dead. In other words, they are the singular place upon the face of the Earth that God has authorized us to perform sacred and exalting ordinances on behalf of those who are currently being taught (in the spirit world) the restored gospel of Jesus Christ. Thus, temples are established not only for the salvation of the living but also for the salvation of our dead.

On a related note, the temple is a place of charity and service. Within the walls of the temple, we serve the living and the dead. We go there to do for the deceased what they cannot do for themselves, namely, to enter into sacred covenants on their behalf by performing ordinances (like baptisms for the dead, endowments, and sealings) in their names. We also go there to help the living who have challenges in their lives, praying for them, so that difficulties in their lives might be alleviated. As we attend the temple regularly, we learn to serve and love others—including those whom we have never met. Jesus commanded, "Thou shalt love thy neighbor as thyself" (D&C 59:6). The temple helps us learn how to do that.

Sister Ardeth G. Kapp (b. 1931), the ninth General President of the Church's Young Women organization, called the holy temple "the university of the Lord."[3] The Lord Himself has spoken of the temple as "a house of learning" (D&C 88:119). Truly, temples are places where we can receive divine instruction. There we learn not only about the purpose of life, the doctrine of the gospel, and the dangers of the adversary but also about what aspects of this mortal experience are *really* of eternal importance. As Latter-day Saint scholar Hugh Nibley (1910–2005) once noted, "The temple is . . . a sort of observatory where one gets one's bearings on the universe."[4] It is the place we go to figure out who we are and what our relationship to God—and others—is.

Finally, the temple is a place where we can go to contemplate the covenants we've made. We cannot keep covenants we do not understand. Thus, the temple affords us the chance to hear recited again and again the covenants we have made. Through participating in temple ordinances, our covenants become clearer to us, and they sink down deeply into our hearts, and we thereby are better able to keep the promises we have made with God. That makes it possible for Him to more richly bless us.

Notes

1. Russell M. Nelson, *Hope in Our Hearts* (Salt Lake City, UT: Deseret Book, 2009), 36, 35, and 34.

2. Ezra Taft Benson, *The Teachings of Ezra Taft Benson* (Salt Lake City, UT: Bookcraft, 1998), 538.

3. Ardeth G. Kapp, "Fruits of Faith," in *The Lectures on Faith in Historical Perspective* (Provo, UT: Religious Studies Center, Brigham Young University, 1990), 279.

4. Hugh Nibley, "Meanings and Functions of Temples," in *Encyclopedia of Mormonism*, Daniel H. Ludlow, ed., four volumes (New York: Macmillan, 1994), 4:1458.

2

Why is it important that we make covenants in the temple?

Before discussing *why* we make covenants in the temple, it may be helpful to explain *what* a covenant is. The Church has offered the following definition of covenants:

> A covenant is often defined as a sacred promise between God and His children. While this definition is accurate, it is not complete. A covenant is more than a contract; it is a personal commitment that defines and deepens our relationship with God. Covenants form a sacred bond between God and His children. They renew our spirits, change our hearts, and help us become united with Him. As you remain faithful to your covenants, your devotion to Heavenly Father and Jesus Christ will increase. Your feelings of gratitude will swell. Your capacity to love and serve others will grow. And the blessings promised in the temple will flow into your everyday life more abundantly. . . .
>
> Through covenants, God helps us understand principles, practices, and promises that He deems are important. We can certainly gain a more inspired perspective on priorities and make wiser choices when we focus first on those sacred commitments we have made with God. . . .
>
> As you prepare to participate in temple ordinances, remember that God is your Eternal Father and Jesus Christ your Redeemer. They know you personally. They love you completely. As you faithfully honor your covenants with Them, the sacred temple ordinances will provide blessings in this life and the next.[1]

Covenants are protective and empowering. They are promises we make to God that offer us incomprehensible blessings *if* we keep them. The covenants you make in the temple will help you deepen your relationship with God, help you feel His power more readily in your life, protect you from temptation and sin, and help you keep in perspective what really matters—particularly in tempting or trying times. Thus, the Prophet Joseph Smith (1805–1844) taught that you *need* temple ordinances and covenants "in order that you may be prepared and able to overcome all things."[2] It is important that we make covenants in the temple, because those covenants will protect and strengthen us against our trials and temptations. Moreover, they will also enable us to overcome the world, and thereby become like God—so that we can do what God does throughout eternity. Perhaps this is one reason why we make certain covenants *only in the temple*. The covenants of the temple require a higher degree of faithfulness and commitment than those we make outside of the temple. Because the temple has high standards for entrance, making certain covenants in the temple requires that we first spiritually prepare ourselves for what we are about to commit to. In that process of preparation, we also develop the spiritual strength to face the temptations and trials that life will throw our way—and to keep the very covenants we will make when we enter the holy temple. President Boyd K. Packer (1924–2015), former President of the Quorum of the Twelve Apostles, explained:

> *Ordinances and covenants become our credentials for admission into [God's] presence.* To worthily receive them is the quest of a lifetime; to keep them thereafter is the challenge of mortality.
>
> Once we have received them for ourselves and for our families, we are obligated to provide these ordinances vicariously for our kindred dead, indeed for the whole human family. . . .
>
> The Lord did for us what we could not do for ourselves. Is it not Christlike for us to perform in the temples ordinances for and in behalf of those who cannot do them for themselves?[3]

I love this idea; our covenants—if kept—become our "credentials for admission" into the celestial kingdom. They are our passports into God's presence. Our covenants are what make it possible for us to return to God, even though we have struggled during our lives with sin. In making covenants, we promise God that we will *try* to be obedient and faithful. By covenant, God then promises us that He will accept our *efforts* at obedience and faithfulness by forgiving our sins and failings. In other words, our covenants are the agreement through which we gain salvation. We promise to *try* to be like God, and He promises to make up the difference when we fall short.

Notes

1. "Prepare for the Temple: Make Your Experience More Personal and Meaningful," https://www.lds.org/temples/prepare-for-your-temple-visit.
2. Joseph Smith, *Teachings of the Prophet Joseph Smith*, Joseph Fielding Smith, compiler (Salt Lake City, UT: Deseret Book, 1976), 91.
3. Boyd K. Packer, "Covenants," *Ensign*, May 1987, 24, emphasis added.

3

Why is it important to do ordinances for our dead ancestors?

In his vision of the redemption of the dead, President Joseph F. Smith (1838–1918), sixth President of the Church, learned that the dead residing in the spirit world felt as if they were "captives who were bound" until they received the gospel there and had their temple ordinances performed for them (see D&C 138:31, 58). Receiving those ordinances gives them both a sense of freedom from spiritual bondage and an ability to be used by God to further the work of the kingdom there in the spirit world.

In Obadiah 1:21, we read, "And saviours shall come up on mount Zion." The phrase "mount Zion" is traditionally seen as a symbol for the holy temple.[1] Thus, here the Lord speaks of "saviors" or helpers who would come to the temple to assist in the redemption of the dead. You and I—if we have taken upon ourselves sacred covenants—are commanded to become saviors on mount Zion so that the dead who are "captives" in the spirit world may be freed from their spiritual bondage. The Prophet Joseph Smith (1805–1844) explained:

> But how are they to become saviors on Mount Zion? By building their temples, erecting their baptismal fonts, and going forth and receiving all the ordinances, baptisms, confirmations, washings, anointings, ordinations and sealing powers upon their heads, in behalf of all their progenitors who are dead, and redeem them that they may come forth in the first resurrection and be exalted to thrones of glory with them; and herein is the chain that binds the hearts of the fathers to the children, and the children to the fathers, which fulfills the mission of Elijah.[2]

14

Doing temple work is, in a way, acting as Jesus acted. He worked to save the spiritually dead, while He also redeemed the physically dead. When you and I act as saviors on Mount Zion, serving in the temple, we seek to help in the redemption of the physically dead and we also pray for the salvation of the spiritually dead. President Russell M. Nelson (b. 1924), seventeenth President of the Church, has taught, "By doing for others what they cannot do for themselves, we emulate the pattern of the Savior, who wrought the Atonement to bless the lives of other people."[3]

In Doctrine and Covenants 128:15, we find emphasized the dual purpose of ordinance work performed on behalf of the dead in the house of the Lord: "And now my dearly beloved brethren and sisters, let me assure you that these are principles in relation to the dead and the living that cannot be lightly passed over, as pertaining to our salvation. For their salvation is necessary and essential to our salvation, as Paul says concerning the fathers—that they without us cannot be made perfect—neither can we without our dead be made perfect." Here we learn that temple work accomplishes two things; it saves the living while it saves the dead. How does it save the living? As you and I do the work that the dead cannot do for themselves (e.g., baptisms, confirmations, endowments, sealings, etc.), we are sanctified. We are changed. We are made more holy and loving. We are forgiven of sins that we may have committed. We better understand our covenants and are more able to keep the commandments. We become more Christlike, more spiritual, more faithful, more patient, more compassionate, and more capable of enduring *any* trial that comes our way. Thus, as we seek to offer saving ordinances to our deceased ancestors who reside in the spirit world, we become like God ourselves—and we increase the likelihood that we will inherit the celestial kingdom when we die. In saving our dead, we actually help to save ourselves.

Notes

1. See D. Kelly Ogden and Andrew C. Skinner, *Verse By Verse: The Old Testament—Volume Two, 1 Kings Through Malachi* (Salt Lake City, UT: Deseret Book, 2013), 339.
2. Joseph Smith, *Teachings of the Prophet Joseph Smith*, Joseph Fielding Smith, compiler (Salt Lake City, UT: Deseret Book, 1976), 330.
3. Russell M. Nelson, *Hope in Our Hearts* (Salt Lake City, UT: Deseret Book, 2009), 108.

4

What are the different ordinances performed in the temple?

A number of sacred ordinances are performed in the holy temple. The most important ones for you to know about at this point are these:

- *Baptisms*—While we *do not* currently do baptisms on behalf of the living in the temple, we *do* perform vicarious baptisms on behalf of deceased individuals therein. These deceased, disembodied persons, now dwelling in the spirit world, are able to accept or reject the vicarious baptisms performed on their behalf, as they can do for any of the temple ordinances performed on their behalf. If they accept their baptism and the other ordinances performed for them, this puts them in a covenant relationship with God, makes them a member of His true Church, and affords them various rights, privileges, and blessings reserved for those who have entered into sacred covenants.

- *Confirmations*—Just as the living (after being baptized) are confirmed members of The Church of Jesus Christ of Latter-day Saints and are given the gift of the Holy Ghost, we also perform vicarious confirmations in the temple for those spirits who are in the spirit world. This gives them access to the gift of the Holy Ghost, and also to various gifts of the Spirit that they may need in their work of preaching the gospel and administering the affairs of God's kingdom in the spirit world.

- *Ordinations*—All deceased males for whom we perform temple ordinances need to have vicariously conferred upon them the Melchizedek Priesthood prior to receiving their temple endowment. Each is ordained to the office of elder.

◆ *Washings and Anointings*—The washing and anointing ordinances are sometimes referred to as the "initiatory" ordinances of the temple. The word *initiatory* means "beginning," and these washing and anointing ordinances are technically the beginning portion of the endowment. A version of these ordinances was called the "endowment" in the Kirtland Temple.[1] (You can read more about "washings and anointings" in Question #25.)

◆ *Endowments*—The temple endowment is the longest and most detailed of the ordinances we perform in the house of the Lord. It is during the endowment that the majority of temple covenants are entered into. In addition, out of the various ordinances performed in temples today, it is during the endowment ceremony that the greatest amount of doctrine is taught.

◆ *Sealings*—In the temple, we seal (or bind for eternity) husbands to wives and children to parents. For couples who were sealed in the temple *before* having children, their offspring are "born in the covenant" and need not have a sealing to their parents performed after they are born. (In Question #36, you will find more information on what it means to be "born in the covenant.")

Note

1. See "anoint" and "washing," in Andrew H. Hedges et al., eds., *Journals, Volume 3: May 1843–June 1844*, vol. 3 of the Journals series of *The Joseph Smith Papers*, ed. Ronald K. Esplin and Matthew J. Grow (Salt Lake City: Church Historian's Press, 2015), 478 & 490.

5

Are the ordinances we perform in temples today the same as those performed in temples anciently?

The needs of the Saints in one dispensation may not be the same as those in another dispensation. Even from generation to generation, needs may vary, and thus ordinances might look somewhat different.

As an example, Moroni 4:2 states that the Nephite priests and *the entire congregation* did kneel during the sacrament prayers. However, in the New Testament, Jesus appears to have offered the sacrament while He and His Apostles were reclining around a table (Luke 22:14–20). In the days of the Prophet Joseph, though, it was not uncommon for a sermon to be delivered while the sacrament was being passed. In the early twentieth century, music would be played while the sacrament was administered—and that continued to be the case until 1946. Today, of course, only the priest saying the prayer kneels, and no music or preaching takes place while the sacrament is being distributed.[1]

Like the ordinance of the sacrament, the ordinances of the temple have not been identical in every dispensation nor in every generation. In Moses's day, temple worship was heavily focused on animal sacrifices as reminders of Christ's death on our behalf. Today, no such blood sacrifices take place in the temples of the Church. Similarly, in the days of Joseph Smith and Brigham Young, it is claimed that it took as much as eight hours to participate in the endowment ceremony.[2] Today it takes less than two hours.

In my book *Sacred Symbols: Finding Meaning in Rites, Rituals, and Ordinances*, I show that many things we do in Latter-day Saint temples today were certainly practiced in previous centuries. However, we should not assume that what Moses did in the tabernacle would be exactly the same as what Paul did in Herod's temple, nor should we assume that either of these would be identical to what we do in Latter-day Saint temples today. The Prophet Joseph Smith once said, "That which is wrong under one circumstance, may be, and often is, right under another."[3] What Moses's people needed would be wrong for us today, and what we need today is not what the ancients needed.

Though we believe that all saving ordinances will need to be performed for each of God's children, we recognize that the way God "packaged" those ordinances and covenants in one dispensation may be different from how He presented them in another. The First Presidency of the Church has stated:

> Whenever the Lord has had a people on the earth who will obey His word, they have been commanded to build temples. Scriptures document patterns of temple worship from the times of Adam and Eve, Moses, Solomon, Nephi, and others.
>
> With the restoration of the gospel in these latter days, temple worship has also been restored to bless the lives of people across the world and on the other side of the veil as well.
>
> *Over these many centuries, details associated with temple work have been adjusted periodically,* including language, methods of construction, communication, and record-keeping. *Prophets have taught that there will be no end to such adjustments as directed by the Lord to His servants.*[4]

Thus, while temple worship has been different in each dispensation, what haven't changed over the millennia are the priesthood keys by which the exalting ordinances are performed. In *every* dispensation, God has restored keys of the priesthood to govern the affairs of His kingdom and to ensure that the ordinances performed in His holy name are valid for time and for all eternity.

Notes

1. See James B. Allen, "*I Have a Question*: I'm puzzled by the instructions in D&C 20:76 that the priests should 'kneel with the church' in blessing the sacrament. What does this mean, and has it ever been the practice for the whole congregation to kneel?," in *Ensign*, March 1978, 23.

2. See Hubert Howe Bancroft, *The Works of Hubert Howe Bancroft, Volume XXVI, History of Utah—1540–1886* (San Francisco, CA: The History Company, 1889), 357, note 17.

3. Joseph Smith, *Teachings of the Prophet Joseph Smith*, Joseph Fielding Smith, compiler (Salt Lake City, UT: Deseret Book, 1976), 255.

4. "First Presidency Statement on Temples," January 2, 2019. https://www. mormonnewsroom.org/article/temple-worship, emphasis added. See also Russell M. Nelson, *Accomplishing The Impossible: What God Does—What We Can Do* (Salt Lake City, UT: Deseret Book, 2015), 63.

6

Why do some people say that what they experienced in the temple was "weird"?

Latter-day Saint Sunday worship is not very symbolic or ritualistic. True, we have the ordinance of the sacrament, where the priest symbolizes Jesus, the white sacrament cloths remind us of purity and holiness, and the bread and water symbolize the Savior's broken body and spilt blood on our behalf. However, beyond that, our typical Sunday experience is not very symbolic or ceremonial.

There are other symbolic experiences we engage in during our various worship services, such as when a group of priesthood holders encircles a baby to give it a name and a blessing, when we enter into the baptismal font to be baptized, or when hands are laid upon our head to confirm or bless us. Though these ordinances are saturated in symbolism, many of us don't think as deeply about the meaning of the symbols in these ordinances as we ought to. Indeed, those who are born in the Church sometimes struggle to think symbolically because their typical experiences with church aren't heavily symbolic.

That being said, the temple is the exact opposite. Pretty much *everything* about the temple is symbolic. The architecture, the art, the clothing, the gestures we make with our bodies, and the way we enter into covenants are all *heavily* symbolic (see Question #51). Consequently, if you aren't versed in symbolism—which many members aren't—then your first encounter with the temple can feel very foreign and, for some, even a bit weird. Thus, the symbolism tends to be the challenge for many. President David O. McKay (1873–1970), ninth President of the Church, expressed concern that "there are very few people in the Church who comprehend" the meaning of the ordinances of the temple.[1]

To a group of young missionaries who were about to receive their endowment, President McKay said:

I have met so many young people who have been disappointed after they have gone through the House of the Lord. They have been honest in that disappointment. Some of them have . . . expressed heart-felt sorrow that they did not see and hear and feel what they had hoped to see and hear and feel.

I have analyzed those confessions as I have listened to them, and I have come to the conclusion that in nearly every case . . . he or she has failed to comprehend the significance of the message that is given in the temple. . . .

These young people . . . have become absorbed in what I am going to call the "mechanics" of the Temple, and while criticizing these they have failed to get the *spiritual* significance.[2]

President McKay noted that when he received his own endowment as a young man he, too, didn't have a very good experience. He explained why:

Do you remember when you first went through the House of the Lord? I do. And I went out disappointed. Just a young man, out of college, anticipating great things when I went to the Temple. I was disappointed and grieved, and I have met hundreds of young men and young women since who had that experience. I have now found out why. There are two things in every Temple: *mechanics*, to set forth certain ideals, and *symbolism*, what those mechanics symbolize. I saw only the mechanics when I first went through the Temple. I did not see the spiritual [meaning behind the mechanics]. I did not see the symbolism of spirituality. Speaking plainly, I saw men, [in their] physical state, which offended me. [For example, there] is a mechanic of washing [in the temple]. . . . I was blind to the great lesson of purity behind the mechanics. I did not hear the message of the Lord, "By ye clean who bear the vessels of the Lord." I did not hear that eternal truth, "Cleanliness is next to godliness." The symbolism was lost entirely. . . . And so [also] with the

23

anointing, [which we do] following the washing. Do you see the symbolism? . . . How many of us young men saw that? We thought we were big enough and with intelligence sufficient to criticize the mechanics of it and we were [actually] blind to the symbolism, [and to] the message of the spirit [of the temple].[3]

President McKay also pointed out that "every word, and nearly every act in life serves two purposes."[4] A word "denotes something" (its primary meaning) and it "connotes other things" (its attributes aside from the word's primary meaning). So, for example, the word "winter" *denotes* a season of the year. However, that same word typically *connotes* chilly weather. When participating in temple ordinances, one must *not* focus solely on the *denotation* (primary meaning) of the words and actions but also contemplate the *connotation* (or symbolic implication) of the words and acts utilized or displayed.

The basic point President McKay was making is that those who think the temple is weird are not getting what the symbolism means. If you understand the symbolism—and if you don't take literally that which is intended symbolically—then it won't seem weird at all. However, if you focus on the "mechanics" of what is going on in the temple, and not on the symbolic meaning behind those "mechanics" (e.g., the clothing, the gestures, the stories told), then you will totally miss the point of what is being taught—and you'll probably then feel like the experience is foreign or weird. As I have personally interacted with Latter-day Saints across the world and have talked with some who did not enjoy their temple experience (even to the degree that some have not returned after they were endowed), almost without exception, the reason was their symbolic illiteracy.

I appreciate the way Adam Miller explains the seeming strangeness of the temple experience. He writes:

Where our churches are simple and spare, our temples are layered with murals, carvings, and symbols. Where our churches are down-to-earth and plainspoken, our temples are filled with allusions, allegories, and sacred gestures. Growing up in the warm, shallow pools of our Sunday services may do little to prepare you for the temple's deep and bracing waters. Compared to the worn predictability of our Sunday School lessons, many members first find the temple strange. I suppose this is as it should be. The temple *is* strange. It does not belong to this world. The temple is a door, and if you pass through it, you will arrive someplace you've never been. The aim of the temple is to initiate you into the mysteries of the kingdom, and before you can solve these mysteries you must encounter them as just that: unsolved mysteries.

Unveiling the mysteries of the kingdom, the temple will initiate you into what you do not know. It will acquaint you with your own ignorance. It will, with little explanation, commend to your care a series of undeciphered stories and symbols that you must neither dismiss nor explain but keep.[5]

We go to the temple seeking the "mysteries of godliness"—but then, when we encounter them, some are put off by the fact that they were "mysterious." Yet isn't that how mysteries should be? If what we encounter in the temple is supposed to be God's higher knowledge and higher ordinances, then should this not be different from the mundane everyday things we know so well, different from those things that feel so familiar to us? The temple is different from what we know *because* it is introducing us to something new, deeper, and ultimately profound. Do not be put off by the differentness of the ordinances of the temple. Rather, seek to "decipher" the "undeciphered" mysteries offered to you in the house of the Lord. If you pay a price to figure out what it is God is trying to share with you through these more esoteric symbolic ordinances, I can promise you that the blessings and insights you will gain will be worth all of the effort you had to put forth in order to lay hold on them. (In Question #73, I will suggest some resources that will help you understand the symbolism after you have made your first trip through the temple.)

Notes

1. David O. McKay, cited in Gregory A. Prince and William Robert Wright, *David O. McKay and the Rise of Modern Mormonism* (Salt Lake City, UT: University of Utah Press, 2001), 277.

2. David O. McKay, "An Address on the Temple Ceremony," given to missionaries at the Salt Lake Temple Annex, Thursday, September 25, 1941. Harold B. Lee Library, Special Collections, Brigham Young University. P.1. President McKay addressed these remarks to missionaries *prior* to their receiving their endowments—and *not* actually in the temple itself, but in the annex next to the temple. See also Truman G. Madsen, *The Radiant Life* (Salt Lake City, UT: Bookcraft, 1994), 125–126.

3. David O. McKay, cited in Gregory A. Prince and William Robert Wright, *David O. McKay and the Rise of Modern Mormonism* (Salt Lake City, UT: University of Utah Press, 2001), 277, emphasis added.

4. McKay (1941), 1.

5. Adam S. Miller, *Letters to a Young Mormon*, second edition (Salt Lake City, UT: Deseret Book and the Maxwell Institute, 2007), 87–88.

7

Why does the Lord use symbols so heavily in the temple?

There is no question that symbolism in its various forms is intentionally present in scripture. Indeed, symbolism is the language of scripture. To not be versed in symbolism is to be scripturally illiterate. The same could be said of the temple and its ordinances. "Symbols are the language in which *all* gospel covenants and *all* ordinances of salvation have been revealed. From the time we are immersed in the waters of baptism to the time we kneel at the altar of the temple with the companion of our choice in the ordinance of eternal marriage, *every* covenant we make will be written in the language of symbolism."[1] Similarly, President Russell M. Nelson (b. 1924), seventeenth President of the Church, has taught:

> Each temple is a house of learning (D&C 88:119; 109:8). There we are taught in the Master's way. His way differs from the modes of others. His way is ancient and rich with symbolism. We can learn much by pondering the reality for which each symbol stands. Teachings of the temple are beautifully simple and simply beautiful. They are understood by the humble, yet they can excite the intellect of the brightest minds.[2]

Indeed, the ordinances of the temple are heavily laden with symbolism. Almost everything that is done, and certainly everything that is worn in the temple, has symbolic meaning (see questions 23, 25, 31–33, 42–43, 47, 50–51, 54, 56, 58–59, and 73–74). The way we make covenants in the temple is symbolic. The way we tell the story of the Creation and the Fall in the temple is symbolic.[3] Even the architecture of the building is symbolic. President Harold B. Lee (1899–1973), eleventh President of the Church—in speaking to a group of missionaries about the temple—said this: "Sisters and Elders, . . . I feel impressed to share with you an idea. None of the things you see portrayed in the ceremony [of the endowment] actually took place that way. They are all symbols: symbols of your life's spiritual journey."[4] President Lee's point was that we must not take literally that which is intended symbolically. We must see beyond the symbols in order to find the intended meaning.

In His holy house, the Lord intentionally uses symbolism as a teaching device. It is important for us to understand that if we are to understand what He is trying to reveal to us. Of course, there are a number of possible reasons why the Lord chooses to use symbols when He instructs us in the temple. Here are some likely explanations for the extensive symbolism used in the house of the Lord.

First, symbols require effort in the form of contemplation and, to some degree, searching. Thus, their employment in the temple encourages us to ponder what we are experiencing there, to fully participate in the rite at hand. If we are willing to pay the price, this attitude of searching and reflection will be rewarded through the receipt of new discoveries, previously unknown insights, and a significantly deepened love for the temple.

Second, symbols are designed to protect the sacred—revealing to those who are prepared, while concealing from the unworthy or unprepared. Elder Bruce R. McConkie (1915–1985), of the Quorum of the Twelve Apostles, wrote:

> Our Lord used *parables* on frequent occasions during his ministry to teach gospel truths. His purpose, however, in telling these short stories was *not* to present the truths of his gospel in plainness so that all his hearers would understand. Rather it was so to phrase and hide the doctrine involved that only the spiritually literate would understand it, while those whose understandings were darkened would remain in darkness. (Matt. 13:10–17; JST, Matt. 21:34)[5]

Through His use of symbols in the temple, the Lord is able to reveal to us what we need to know when we are truly ready to receive and use that knowledge. What we are not ready for, He can easily conceal through the symbols used in the temple.

A third reason why temple ordinances might be so saturated in symbolism is that many symbols are timeless, meaning many translate well from language to language, culture to culture, and age to age. For example, a lamb has a fairly universal association with innocence, gentleness, meekness, and purity. Blood, on the other hand, is usually a negative symbol, and is traditionally associated with death, guilt, impurity, sin, the need for atonement, and so on. Because of the timelessness of symbols, God can use the same symbol to teach His children in any nation and potentially in any dispensation.

A fourth potential reason for temple symbolism is the reality that symbols have a tremendous ability to impact the mind and create lasting impressions. Once one has attached a specific meaning to a given symbol, any future encounter of that symbol will bring a resurgence of thoughts or feelings associated with the assigned meaning. Perhaps one of the most universal examples of this reality is found in the sign of the cross. Although the majority of the world's inhabitants do not use the cross as a religious symbol, nevertheless, most people instantly associate it with Christianity, and nearly all Christians see it as a reminder of Christ's sacrifice on their behalf.

A fifth reason why symbols are so helpful in temple worship is the fact that they are multi-layered. In other words, they provide numerous levels of understanding, contingent upon one's level of spiritual maturity or understanding. Thus, President Boyd K. Packer (1924–2015), former President of the Quorum of the Twelve Apostles, wrote, "The temple ordinances . . . have different meanings to the young [than they do] to the old."[6] One author explained:

> Symbols are the language of feeling, and as such, it is not expected that everyone will perceive them in the same way.

Like a beautifully cut diamond, they catch the light and then reflect its splendor in a variety of ways. As viewed at different times and from different positions, what is reflected will differ, yet the diamond and the light remain the same. Thus symbols, like words, gain richness in their variety of meanings and purposes, which range from revealing to concealing great gospel truths.[7]

Because of the multilayered nature of symbols, they can continue to teach you new things throughout your entire life. At one point, a given temple symbol will mean one thing to you. Years later, it may have a much deeper and more profound meaning to you. Thus, you don't need to worry as much about what a given symbol means as you do about what it means for *you* at the current stage of your life.

Sixth, symbols can spark interest or curiosity. They can make the otherwise mundane seem fresh and interesting. By blanketing the covenants of the temple in symbols, the Lord has made them more palatable, more interesting and curious—a potentially important choice, owing to the fact that you and I will most likely hear those covenants recited hundreds, if not thousands, of times over a lifetime of temple service.

As a seventh and final point, one of the great values of symbols is their ability to functionally teach abstract concepts. For example, bread (as a symbol for Christ) teaches well the abstract idea that Jesus, His gospel, and its teachings, *must* become a part of our very being if we are to be exalted in the celestial kingdom of God. The concept of Jesus or the gospel "becoming part of us" is abstract and potentially hard to grasp. However, using bread as a symbol of this idea actually serves to clarify. For, just as the bread we eat is broken down and becomes part of our bodies, thereby sustaining us and strengthening us, so also Christ, His gospel, and His teachings *must* become a part of us, if they are to strengthen us and sustain us eternally.

Elder John A. Widtsoe (1872–1952), of the Quorum of the Twelve Apostles, pointed out, "We live in a world of symbols. No man or woman can come out of the temple *endowed as he should be*, unless he has seen beyond the symbol, the mighty realities for which the symbols stand."[8] Thus, we really *do* need to understand the symbols we encounter therein. This will take time; it will take effort on our behalf. "The temple experience will not be understood at first experience."[9] However, as we earnestly study, contemplate, and pray about what we experience in the temple, the Lord will reveal to us what it is that *He* wants us to understand about a given symbol we encounter in the temple. Over time, as we mature, and as we have different needs in our life, God may show us new things about or different meanings of the symbols we felt we already understood. That is exactly as it should be (see point five above). This evolution in our understanding of the meaning of the symbols will enable them to constantly teach us new things, but it will also keep our experience fresh so that we never need to be bored by what we encounter in the house of the Lord. As President Boyd K. Packer explained, "As we grow and mature and learn from all of the experiences in life, the truths demonstrated in the temple in symbolic fashion take on a renewed meaning. The veil is drawn back a little bit more. Our knowledge and vision of the eternities expands. It is always refreshing."[10]

Notes

1. Joseph Fielding McConkie and Donald W. Parry, *A Guide to Scriptural Symbols*, (Salt Lake City, UT: Bookcraft, 1990), 1, emphasis added.
2. Russell M. Nelson, *Hope in Our Hearts* (Salt Lake City, UT: Deseret Book, 2009), 106.
3. Ed J. Pinegar, *The Temple: Gaining Knowledge and Power in the House of the Lord* (American Fork, UT: Covenant Communications, 2014), 12.
4. Harold B. Lee, cited in Thomas B. Griffith, "Imagination and the Temple," in *Brigham Young University Humanities: Think Clearly, Act Well, Appreciate Life*, Spring 2018, 24. I express appreciation to Elder Marlin K. Jensen, emeritus member of the First Quorum of the Seventy and former Church Historian, for bringing this source to my attention.
5. Bruce R. McConkie, *Mormon Doctrine*, second edition (Salt Lake City, UT: Bookcraft, 1979), 553, emphasis in original.
6. Boyd K. Packer, *The Holy Temple* (Salt Lake City, UT: Bookcraft, 1980), 259.
7. Joseph Fielding McConkie, *Gospel Symbolism* (Salt Lake City, UT: Bookcraft, 1985), ix.

8. John A. Widtsoe, "Temple Worship," in *The Utah Genealogical and Historical Magazine* Vol. 12 (April 1921): 62, emphasis added.
9. Boyd K. Packer, *The Holy Temple* (Salt Lake City, UT: Bookcraft, 1980), 41.
10. Boyd K. Packer, *The Holy Temple* (Salt Lake City, UT: Bookcraft, 1980), 39.

8

Is it true that Satan will try to discourage me from participating in temple work?

Although everyone's experience is different, many people have borne witness that when they committed to be baptized, when they decided to receive the Melchizedek Priesthood or to serve a full-time mission, or when they determined that they wanted to enter the temple, Satan tried very hard to keep that from happening. Challenges arose, obstacles were placed in their path, or friends and family members protested.

Why would the devil do something like this? Well, the gospel is true, isn't it? Certainly every time you seek to do something that is right or good or that will move you closer to exaltation, Satan is going to be upset with you, and he is going to do everything within his power to stop you. Consequently, if you are one of those people who experience opposition when you are preparing to receive your endowment or be sealed in the temple, take that as a good sign that what you are doing is right and true and that Satan's kingdom feels threatened by your faithfulness. You may recall the words of the Prophet Joseph Smith (1805–1844), who noted, "It seems as though the adversary was aware, at a very early period of my life, that I was destined to prove a disturber and an annoyer of his kingdom; else why should the powers of darkness combine against me? Why the opposition and persecution that arose against me, almost in my infancy?" (JS—H 1:20). If you, too, experience opposition, as the Prophet did, know that it is simply evidence that you are on the right team! The devil may rage and oppose your decision. However, if you remain faithful to what you know is right, he will eventually realize that he cannot deter you from the temple.

What You Must Do before You Go to the Temple

❧ *9* ❧

How will I know if I am ready
to enter the temple?

There are several things that will help you to know when the
right time is for you to attend the temple and make the higher
covenants offered therein.

Perhaps the first thing you should ask yourself is, "Am I doing
this because this is something *I want,* or because I'm getting pres-
sure from someone else to go to the temple?" If you feel the Spirit
urging you to go, that is a good sign that you should be preparing
yourself to enter the temple and make sacred covenants. If, on the
other hand, you are really only thinking about going because a
parent, spouse, bishop, or other leader is pushing you to, it might be
best to wait and perhaps take a temple preparation course instead.
That might actually help you to gain a stronger testimony that this
is something you need and want in your life.

Another set of questions worth asking yourself (as you contemplate receiving your endowment) is

+ Am I spiritually mature?
+ Do I keep the covenants I made at baptism?
+ Do I faithfully fulfill my callings?
+ Am I ready for an even bigger commitment to the Lord and His
  Church?

If you can honestly answer *yes* to each of these questions, you're
most likely ready for the commitments you will make in the temple
(see Question #38).

An important question to ask yourself before participating in
any temple ordinance is "Am I worthy to enter the house of the

Lord?" It is important to be spiritually clean and worthy when you attend the temple, not only because it makes a mockery of God and His ordinances to enter into covenants unworthily but also because you will not feel the Spirit during your temple experience if you are not worthy. That will leave you with a hollow or empty feeling. It may also cause you to misunderstand some of what you will experience in the temple. Thus, being worthy is very important. Of course, if you are not currently worthy, seek out your bishop. You may not realize it, but he loves you and can walk you through the repentance process so that you can be clean again, and so that you can go to the temple and enjoy both the Spirit there and the power offered to those who worthily attend.

One of the reasons you will have an interview with your bishop (or branch president) and stake (or mission) president *before* participating in the ordinances of the temple is so that they—having the gift of discernment—can help determine if you are ready to make the higher covenants of the temple (Luke 12:48; D&C 82:3). As they interview you, those two inspired men will ask you questions that will help both you and them know if the time is right for you to make and keep additional sacred covenants.

10

What must I do to obtain
a temple recommend?

If you wish to attend the temple, you will need to first have at least two interviews in order to obtain a temple recommend (see Question #11). The *Encyclopedia of Mormonism* states, "All who enter the temple must come as worthy members duly certified by ecclesiastical leaders—the Bishop and the Stake President."[1] If you live in a branch (instead of a ward) or a district (instead of a stake), your branch president and mission president will conduct these interviews.

If you are seeking a recommend to participate only in baptisms for the dead, you will need to be interviewed by your bishop or one of his counselors. You will not, however, need to be interviewed by the stake president to receive a limited-use recommend to perform baptisms for the dead.

If you are seeking a recommend to receive your endowment or to be married or sealed in the temple, you will need to be interviewed by your bishop (or branch president) and then by your stake president (or the mission president, if you live in a district instead of a stake). The exception to this might be if you live in a single adult stake, where a counselor in the stake presidency (instead of the stake president) *might* interview you before you receive your endowment or before you are sealed in the temple.

In order to schedule these interviews, you will need to call your bishop's (or branch president's) executive secretary. After you have completed the interview, you will need to make an appointment with your stake president's (or mission president's) executive secretary. In both cases, let them know what the interview is about so they will know to schedule ample time for the interview.

If you are a new convert to the Church, you will need to be a member of the Church for at least one year before receiving your endowment. You may also need to wait a year prior to being sealed in the temple, contingent upon when you joined the Church and when you were married. For men, you will need to have received the Melchizedek Priesthood before being endowed or sealed to a spouse in the temple.

New converts desiring to participate in baptisms for the dead can typically do that almost immediately after they are baptized and confirmed a member of the Church. For males, you will need to have received the Aaronic Priesthood before you can participate in baptisms for the dead.

Note

1. Robert L. Simpson, "Administration of Temples," in *Encyclopedia of Mormonism*, Daniel H. Ludlow, ed., four volumes (New York: Macmillan, 1994), 4:1456.

Are there different types of
temple recommends?

There are several types of temple recommends. Contingent upon what ordinances you seek to perform in the temple, there are standard temple recommends, recommends for living ordinances, and limited-use recommends.

Temple Recommend

A standard temple recommend would be issued to a member who is seeking to receive his or her own endowment or who has previously been endowed but whose initial temple recommend has expired or is about to expire. This recommend authorizes its worthy holder to participate in the various ordinances of the temple. (If the person receiving this recommend is planning on being endowed for himself, or sealed to his spouse, he will also need a recommend for living ordinances.)

Recommend for Living Ordinances

A recommend for living ordinances would be issued to a member seeking to receive his or her own endowment in the temple. It would also be issued to a member seeking to be sealed to a spouse. A recommend for living ordinances *must* be accompanied by a valid standard temple recommend (mentioned above) in order for the temple to allow the patron (or attendee) to participate in his or her own endowment or sealing.

Limited-Use Recommend

A limited-use recommend is the type of temple recommend issued to a member who is only seeking to participate in baptisms and confirmations for the dead. You can receive this type of recommend as early as the beginning of the year in which you will turn twelve years of age. (If you are seeking to participate in baptisms and confirmations for the dead, you will only need an interview with your bishop or branch president—or with one of his counselors. You will not need to see a member of the stake or mission presidency in order to participate in these two ordinances.) A limited-use recommend might also be issued to a single member (between the ages of eight and twenty) who has not yet received his or her endowment but who wishes to be sealed to his or her parents. Additionally, a limited-use recommend could be issued to a single member (between the ages of eight and twenty) who has not yet received his or her endowment but who wishes to observe the sealing of his or her living siblings to their parents.

12

What is involved in a temple recommend interview?

When you feel worthy and prepared, you will need to schedule an appointment with your bishop (or branch president) by contacting his executive secretary. Let the executive secretary know that you are seeking a temple recommend, and let him know what kind of recommend you are seeking (as explained in Question #11).

The purpose of this interview is for your bishop—who has been set apart as a common judge in Israel (D&C 107:74)—to ascertain several things about you before sending you to the temple. Many bishops prefer to begin the interview with prayer. Yours may choose to do so also. He may even invite *you* to offer the prayer. Through a series of questions, he will seek to discern whether you have a testimony of the restored gospel of Jesus Christ, if you are worthy to enter the house of the Lord, and if you are spiritually and emotionally ready for the covenants you will be making there. It is important to remember that your bishop loves you and, because of that, you need not feel scared or uncomfortable having this interview.

During your temple recommend interview, you will be asked questions about your testimony and whether you believe in the basic doctrine of the Church (e.g., the Godhead, the Atonement of Jesus Christ, the restoration of the gospel, and living prophets). Your bishop will want to know if you sustain your Church leaders—both the general authorities and the local leaders. He will ask you whether you are keeping the basic commandments of the Church (e.g., the law of chastity, the Word of Wisdom, the law of tithing, treating your family members kindly, being honest, etc.). He will ask you about whether you are active in the Church and whether you are keeping the covenants you have already made. (This is important because if you are not keeping the covenants you made at baptism, you are probably not ready to enter the temple and make additional covenants.) He will probably ask you about whether you have any serious sins that need to be repented of—not because he thinks you are unworthy, but so that you have the opportunity to take care of those things *before* you enter the temple. Your bishop will even ask you if *you* feel you are worthy to attend the temple.[1]

Again, by asking these types of questions, your bishop is simply seeking to discern if now is the right time for you to go to the temple and make additional covenants or promises to God. Your bishop wants you to have a wonderful experience in the temple, and he knows you will *not* have an uplifting or powerful experience if you go unworthily. Therefore, the questions he will be asking you will help him to know how *he* can help you to be most prepared to attend the temple and make sacred covenants.

Once you have completed this interview with your bishop (or branch president), you will then need to contact your stake president's executive secretary (or the mission president's—if you live in a district instead of a stake) to set up an interview with the president. (You will not need to meet with a member of the stake presidency if you are seeking a limited-use recommend to participate in baptisms for the dead.) This interview with your stake (or mission) president will follow the pattern I have described above. You will be asked the same basic questions, and the interview will most likely feel very familiar, since you have just been asked these same questions by your bishop. Most of us do not know our stake presidents as well as we know our bishops, but I can assure you, he too is a kind and loving man who cares deeply about you and who wants you to have a positive experience—both in the temple and in your interview with him.

The reason you will have two very similar interviews and be asked basically the same questions is that this fulfills the Lord's law of witnesses: "In the mouth of two or three witnesses shall every word be established" (Deuteronomy 19:15; Matthew 18:16;

2 Corinthians 13:1; Ether 5:4; D&C 6:28, 128:3). Heavenly Father has established that there be multiple witnesses of sacred things. When we are baptized, there are two witnesses attesting that the baptism was performed correctly. When we receive priesthood blessings, there are typically at least two men standing in the circle exercising their faith on behalf of the person being blessed. When we send out missionaries, we do so two by two that they might both bear witness of the truthfulness of the message that they bear. When a couple is sealed in the temple, there are two witnesses to attest before God that the ordinance was done, and done properly—by proper priesthood authority. And so it is, when *you* testify to your bishop (or branch president) *and* to your stake president (or mission president) that you are worthy to enter the temple and make sacred covenants, you will be testifying to two witnesses who represent the Lord. In effect, you will twice testify to your Father in Heaven (during your temple recommend interviews) that you are worthy to enter His holy house and make sacred covenants with Him.

Note

1.   For a discussion of the types of questions you will be asked in a Temple Recommend interview, see Robert A. Tucker, "Temple Recommend," in *Encyclopedia of Mormonism*, Daniel H. Ludlow, ed., four volumes (New York: Macmillan, 1994), 4:1446.

13

What if I wasn't fully honest in my temple recommend interview?

I had a friend who confided in me that he really didn't like the temple when he first received his endowment. He explained that, in order to obtain a temple recommend, he had lied about his worthiness. He feared that if he confessed his sins (during his recommend interview), he might not be able to serve a full-time mission. Consequently, each time he went to the temple, he felt unworthy to be there, he didn't have the Spirit with him, and he knew that he was defiling God's house because he had lied in order to gain access. It wasn't until he talked to his bishop and resolved the sins that he had lied about that he actually began to feel the Spirit in the temple and could really enjoy being there.

Church officers—such as your bishop, stake president, or their counselors—are commanded by the Lord to make every effort to see that no unworthy person enters the temple. They don't do this to punish those who are struggling with temptations and sin. Rather, they do this so that the sinner can repent and so that the Spirit of the Lord can be unrestrained in the temple.

Doctrine and Covenants 132:7 informs us of a sacred and important principle, a principle that will determine whether the covenants you make in the temple will be acceptable to God. "All covenants, contracts, bonds, obligations, oaths, vows, performances, connections, associations, or expectations, that are not made and entered into and sealed by the Holy Spirit of promise, . . . are of no efficacy, virtue, or force in and after the resurrection from the dead; for all contracts that are not made unto this end have an end when men are dead." What the Lord is suggesting here is that if we enter into covenants but are not worthy to do so, those covenants will not be valid. It will be as though we never made them. This applies to the covenants you made at baptism, to those you renew each week during the sacrament, to those a man makes when he receives the priesthood, and to every covenant we make when we enter the temple. Yes, thankfully, we can repent if we were unworthy when we made those covenants. However, if we do not *sincerely* repent, God will not acknowledge the validity of our baptism, ordination, sealing, or any other ordinance we participated in. Thus, if you were not fully honest with your bishop (or branch president) and stake president (or mission president), you need to set up an interview and let him know. He will not be angry with you. Rather, he will think highly of you for being so humble and willing to repent. He will love you even more for your willingness to do what is right, and the Spirit of the Lord will come upon you—both strengthening you during the interview and helping you to feel acceptable to God and unburdened by sin.

On the subject of being worthy to attend the temple, President Russell M. Nelson (b. 1924), seventeenth President of the Church, has pointed out:

> Inscribed on each temple are the words "Holiness to the Lord" (Exodus 28:36; 39:30; Psalm 93:5). That statement designates both the temple and its purposes as holy. Those who enter the temple are also to bear the attribute of holiness (Exodus 19:5–6; Leviticus 19:1–2; Psalm 24:3–5; 1 Thessalonians 4:7; Moroni 10:32–33; D&C 20:69, 110:6–9). It may be easier to ascribe holiness to a building than to a people. We can acquire holiness only by enduring and persistent personal effort. Through the ages, servants of the Lord have warned against unholiness. . . . As temples are prepared for our members, our members need to prepare for the temple. . . . We cannot cut corners of preparation and risk the breaking of covenants we were not prepared to make. That would be worse than not making them at all.[1]

Similarly, President David O. McKay (1873–1970), ninth President of the Church, asked some young men and young women who were about to receive their endowment, "Are you willing to keep your word? Will you keep your promise made this day? Are you a man or a woman of honor? Will you keep your promise?"[2] If you were not fully honest with your bishop or stake president, you may struggle to be honest with the Lord—you may struggle to keep the covenants you will make in the house of the Lord. You may need some additional time to prepare yourself for the sacred and very serious covenants you are about to make.

It is important to understand that you do not need to be perfect in order to enter or attend the temple. In Doctrine and Covenants 110:7, the Lord states, "For behold, . . . I will manifest myself to my people in mercy in this house." The implication is that those who attend *need* God's mercy. In other words, they are *not* perfect. Obviously, you and I should be striving to live in accordance with the standards set, but perfection is not what is required of us. If all who enter the temple need to be perfect before entering, then they would not need Him to manifest mercy upon them when there. We strive to be holy but also rely upon God's mercy when we fall short.[3] The Lord loves those who repent. If you were less than completely honest in your temple recommend interview, go see your bishop and let him know. Make things right with God, so that the Spirit can be fully present in your life and so that the ordinances you need for salvation will be accepted by God.

Notes

1. Russell M. Nelson, *Hope in Our Hearts* (Salt Lake City, UT: Deseret Book, 2009), 101–102.
2. David O. McKay, "An Address on the Temple Ceremony," given to missionaries at the Salt Lake Temple Annex, Thursday, September 25, 1941. Harold B. Lee Library, Special Collections, Brigham Young University, 3.
3. I express appreciation to Matthew B. Christensen for pointing me to this verse and its application.

14

Is it important to attend a temple preparation class before receiving my endowment?

While the Church does not *require* that you attend a temple preparation course, there is value in being as prepared as possible before you enter the temple, and a temple preparation course can help you in your preparations. A counselor in a temple presidency recently told me that he had noticed that those who had taken a temple preparation course before receiving their endowment were typically better prepared and almost always had a better experience their first time through the temple.

The Church's current temple preparation course, *Endowed from on High: Temple Preparation Seminar*, is not designed to tell you about what you will experience in the temple on the day that you are endowed or sealed. Rather, the focus of the course is to help you to gain a better understanding of the doctrine underlying temple work, and also a stronger testimony that God has revealed these ordinances for the salvation of His sons and daughters here upon the earth.

If your ward or branch does not offer a temple preparation course, approach your bishop (or branch president) and ask about having a member of the ward teach you the lessons before receiving your endowment.

15

How soon after I receive my mission call should I receive my endowment?

The short answer to this question is *immediately*! To members of the Twelve preparing to leave for their missions, the Prophet Joseph Smith (1805–1844) said, "You need an endowment, brethren, in order that you may be prepared and able to overcome all things."[1] The implication of the Prophet's words was that power and knowledge would come into the lives of those who worthily received their endowment. And so it is; the Lord has promised that as we sanctify ourselves, we will be "endowed with power" in the temple (D&C 46:16; see also 38:32, 105:11). However, that power does not come from simply receiving one's endowment. Rather, that power is available to us as we begin to understand the meaning of the ordinances and covenants of the temple. Thus, in order to receive the promised blessing of power, we must spend time in the temple hearing, seeing, doing, and contemplating those sacred things presented there. If a young missionary only goes to the temple once or twice before departing for the mission field, his or her endowment will have limited influence and bring limited power and knowledge. Consequently, those awaiting a mission call should prepare themselves to enter the temple before the receipt of their call so that when the actual mission call arrives, they can immediately receive their endowment.

One of the most common excuses I have heard from young men and young women who have their mission call in hand but have yet to receive their endowment is "I want _____ to be there when I receive my endowment, and they can't come for six more weeks." With all due respect, this is *not* a good reason to wait to receive your endowment. While I am sure that it would be *nice* to have Grandma, Cousin Nell, or your roommate from college in attendance when you receive your endowment, there will be many, many opportunities in the future to attend the temple with them. What is more important *right now* is that you make the very covenants that will save your soul and that you have sufficient time (before departing for your mission) to gain a measure of understanding about what those covenants mean. Provided you remain worthy, you will be able to attend the temple with your parents, grandparents, cousins, and friends throughout the rest of your life. However, once you have your mission call in hand, your next sacred responsibility is to enter the temple and make sacred covenants that will equip you, as the Prophet said, to "be prepared and able to overcome all things."

In addition, for those who live near a temple, if at all possible, attend the temple as many times as is feasible before entering the Missionary Training Center. I realize, of course, some will have to work until nearly the day before they leave in order to save money for their mission. However, most will have time in the evenings or on weekends—or even in the early morning hours, before they go to work—to make regular visits to their local temple. (Some may even be able to serve as an ordinance worker before departing for their mission.) If you live quite some distance from a temple, do the best you can. However, if a temple is fairly near where you live, make the sacrifices necessary to get there as many times as you possibly can before leaving for your mission. This will bless you, and it will bless the dead—including your own ancestors, for whom you may perform temple ordinances. Attending the temple frequently after you receive your mission call, and before you depart for your mission, will greatly increase the likelihood that your endowment will be one of power.

Note

1. Joseph Smith, *Teachings of the Prophet Joseph Smith*, Joseph Fielding Smith, complier (Salt Lake City, UT: Deseret Book, 1976), 91.

16

Do I need to wear church clothes if I am entering the temple?

"Church clothes" or "Sunday best" will vary from nation to nation and place to place. In one country, church clothes might consist of a dress or a suit and tie. In another country, it might consist of a sarong, *lavalava*, or wrap. Elsewhere, it might consist of a collarless shirt and trousers. God is not primarily concerned with what clothes we own or how nicely we are able to dress when we approach Him. He loves and hears us, no matter what our attire is.

That being said, the reason we dress in church clothes or Sunday best when we pay our devotions is that it shows reverence or respect for God and helps us to feel reverent when we engage in worship. President Russell M. Nelson (b. 1924), seventeenth President of the Church, has said, "One prepares physically for the temple by dressing properly. It is not a place for casual attire."[1] Similarly, President Boyd K. Packer (1924–2015), former President of the Quorum of the Twelve Apostles, taught, "Your dress and grooming are signals as to how deeply you revere the privilege of going to the temple. . . . It is a mark of reverence and respect when the Church member visits the temple dressed and groomed in such a way that he would not be uncomfortable in the presence of the Lord."[2] Casual clothes can cause a casual attitude, and they don't really show reverence or respect for the One we profess to worship.

Of course, we should *not* avoid attending the temple simply because we do not feel that we own clothing that is nice enough to be in God's presence. As noted, God will accept you in *whatever* you have. Nevertheless, as we attend the temple, we are encouraged to wear our best (whatever that may be) in an effort to feel a spirit of reverence and in order to make a statement to God that we love and reverence Him and His holy house.

Notes

1. Russell M. Nelson, *Hope in Our Hearts* (Salt Lake City, UT: Deseret Book, 2009), 105.
2. Boyd K. Packer, *The Holy Temple* (Salt Lake City, UT: Bookcraft, 1980), 72. See also p. 74.

17

Do I need to make an appointment to receive my endowment or to be sealed?

Yes, you will need to call the temple well before the day of your endowment or sealing in order to let them know you are coming to receive your ordinances. They will schedule a time for you to attend and will give you instructions on what time you need to arrive, what you will need to bring with you, and what time to tell any family or friends to arrive on the day of your endowment or sealing.

If you plan on receiving your endowment in one of the Church's smaller temples—where patrons need to make an appointment to participate in an endowment session—you will want to let those you wish to be in attendance (at your endowment) know that they too will need to make an appointment with the temple. In many of the smaller temples, an appointment is required of any patron who wishes to participate in a temple ordinance.

18

What if I am worried about not knowing what to do or where to go once I enter the temple? Will there be people available to help me?

A friend of mine told me about how for about the first five years after she received her endowment she worried about not doing something right or not saying something right when she was in the temple. She felt like *everyone* (except her) seemed so sure of what they were supposed to do and where they were supposed to go. However, she simply didn't have that kind of confidence. Finally, she decided to just ask an ordinance worker each time she had a question, and they were always so helpful that she entirely got over her worry about "getting it right." Now she feels quite comfortable in the temple, doesn't worry about somehow messing up, and doesn't hesitate to ask for assistance when she isn't sure about something.

One thing you *never* have to worry about when attending the temple is getting lost, not knowing what to do, or not having help when you need it. Throughout the entire temple are stationed temple workers whose sole job is to answer questions, give directions, and help patrons know what to do, when to do it, and how to do it. So, *relax!* You will have more help than you need, and the ordinance workers are eager to be of assistance to you. If at any point you feel unsure of what to do or where to go, *just ask* one of the numerous ordinance workers standing nearby.

Additionally, just before you receive your endowment, a member of the temple presidency (if you are a male) or one of the temple matrons[1] (if you are female) will sit with you and your escort and give you some instructions. They will usually teach you a bit about the garment you have just received and will instruct you regarding things you are about to experience during the temple endowment. They can answer any questions you have leading up to receiving your endowment.

Note

1. The temple matron and the assistant matrons are the wives of the temple president and his counselors.

Baptism for the Dead

19

How old must I be in order to participate in baptisms for the dead?

Technically, one can enter the temple to participate in the ordinance of baptism for the dead at the beginning of the year in which he or she turns twelve. In addition, young men will need to have had the Aaronic or Melchizedek Priesthood conferred upon them before participating in this ordinance.

That being said, each of us should realize that a vital part of temple work is participating in genealogical research so that names are gathered to be sent to the temple, in order that temple work can be done for those deceased individuals. No baptisms for the dead can be performed if someone doesn't first find the names of the deceased and submit those names that their ordinances might be performed.

Consequently, *well before* a young man or young woman can enter the temple, he or she can engage in family history (genealogical research), finding his or her deceased ancestors—and the deceased ancestors of others—who have yet to receive their temple ordinances. A youth who is computer savvy can compile and submit names that will then be used in temples throughout the world. In so doing, they are participating in the sacred ordinance work of the house of the Lord.

20

What must I take with me to the temple when I go to perform baptisms for the dead?

You really only need to take with you your temple recommend and your testimony when you go to perform baptisms for the dead.

The temple will provide clean, white underwear, white clothing (very similar to what you wore when you were baptized), a towel, and the names of the deceased who need to be baptized and confirmed.

You may wish to take with you a comb or brush of your own for after you are done being baptized for the dead.

Though you are *not* required to bring the names of your own deceased family members when you attend the temple to do baptisms for the dead, if you have some deceased family members who have yet to receive their ordinances, by all means, bring their ordinance cards to the temple with you and be baptized and confirmed for them. Some members feel a special spirit when they are baptized and confirmed for their own deceased ancestors.

⁂ 21 ⁂

How can I best prepare for what I will experience in the temple baptistry?

Each person is different, and how one might prepare will be different from how another might prepare; nevertheless, here are a few things that might be helpful to you as you anticipate attending the temple to perform baptisms for the dead.

Imagine a young woman who is perhaps sixteen or seventeen years of age. She has friends that are Latter-day Saints and has learned from them about the Church. The more she learns about the restored gospel, the more she knows it is true. She feels the Holy Ghost testifying that Jesus is the Christ, that Joseph Smith was a prophet, that the gospel has been restored, and that she needs to be baptized by someone holding God's holy priesthood. She asks her parents for permission to join the Church, but they tell her no. She will not be allowed to be baptized, nor will she be able to attend any of the Church's worship services or activities. She is absolutely devastated! She feels imprisoned by her circumstance. She's overwhelmed by the fact that she knows it is true but isn't able to have the saving ordinance of baptism. She's desperate to make her baptism into the true Church happen and wonders who can help her resolve her dilemma. She would love to serve a full-time mission, but how can she do that if she isn't a member of the Church?

In many ways, this is how the deceased people waiting in the spirit world feel about their circumstance. Many of them have been taught the gospel and absolutely know that it is true. However, they feel imprisoned and powerless. They are stuck in spirit prison because they don't have the saving ordinances they need to enter paradise. So many of them would like to preach the restored gospel (that they have gained a testimony of) to other spirits, but how can they when they are not yet members—when they have yet to enter into the covenant of baptism? Just as the young girl mentioned above wondered who could help free her from her dilemma, many of the spirits in the spirit world wonder who will help them. Who will make their way to the holy temple and perform a baptism on their behalf? Thirty seconds of your time is all it would take to free someone from spirit prison and make it possible for them to be a member of God's true Church. They so desperately want this; many of them have been waiting thousands of years for this opportunity. *You* have the power to free them, to make it possible for them to enter into sacred saving covenants. *You* have the power to make it possible for them to be missionaries in the spirit world.

Thinking deeply about this can help you to prepare for the sacred work you are about to do. It can help you to enter the temple with the right mindset and the right spirit about you. Obadiah 1:21 speaks of "saviours . . . on mount Zion" (see Question #3). As we attend the temple, we act as saviors on mount Zion. We go there and do work for others—work they cannot do for themselves. Knowing that, thinking about that, and thinking about how that will make those on the other side of the veil feel will prepare you to engage in this holy work.

Another thing you can do to prepare to participate in the ordinance of baptism for the dead is to think deeply about the meaning of the covenants you made when *you* were baptized. Thinking about what those covenants should and do mean for you—and thinking about how those covenants apply as much to the dead as they do to you—will help you prepare to be baptized for those who are currently dwelling in the spirit world.

As you are in the temple awaiting your turn to be baptized, spending time thinking about the symbolism of the ordinance, the font, the clothing, and the building can be helpful. Asking yourself, "What is God trying to teach me through all of this?" will help the Holy Ghost to teach you sacred things while you are in the temple. Most of what we do in the temple is symbolic. However, if we do not contemplate the symbolism, we will never *fully* grasp what it is Heavenly Father is trying to say to us.

A very important part of preparing to attend the temple is being worthy to enter the Lord's house. If there are small things in your life that might be keeping you from fully feeling the Spirit, change them so that you will be worthy of the constant companionship of the Holy Ghost. If there are bigger sins you have struggled with—things you should talk with your bishop about—go see him. You may not realize it, but he loves you, and he can help you to take care of these things so that you can enter the temple fully worthy. If you go to the temple spiritually clean and worthy, you will feel the Spirit more strongly there—and others around you will be able to feel the Spirit too. The deceased for whom you will be performing this work deserve to have a worthy young man or young woman represent them at their baptism. This is the only time they will be baptized by proper priesthood authority. We should not dishonor or sully their experience by representing them when we are not clean.

Finally, once you receive your temple recommend, go often. There are so many who are waiting for their ordinances. The more often you go, the more of your brothers and sisters you will save. In addition, as you attend regularly and contemplatively, you will begin to see things that you had not noticed before. You will begin to understand things you didn't understand the first few times you attended. Literally, the more often you attend, the more prepared you will be to come back—and the more ready you will be to receive your endowment, when the time arrives for that.

22

How am I to conduct myself while in the temple?

The holy temple is a sacred place. It is a house of God. More so than our Church buildings, temples invite a *constant* spirit of reverence and respect—both for the God whose house it is and also for the sacred and saving ordinances that take place therein. One of the General Authorities of the Church pointed out that in the temple "all are encouraged to speak with soft voices and guard against extraneous thoughts and conversations, which detract from the spiritual tone of the sanctuary."[1] As we act reverently and think reverent thoughts while in the temple, we increase the likelihood that we will feel God's Spirit and have spiritual experiences while there.

In speaking of the temple, the scriptures counsel us to "cease from all your light speeches, from all laughter, from all your lustful desires, from all your pride and light-mindedness, and from all your wicked doings" (D&C 88:121). This is a good description of how we should behave when we are in the temple. Notice that in this verse the Lord warns us about inappropriate conversations and humor, but also about inappropriate desires and attitudes. While the Lord desires for us to have a pleasant time when we are in His holy house, He also wants us to act in such a way that we do not offend or squelch His Spirit. Thus, the temple is not really a place for joking, laughing, or thinking and talking about worldly things. As we limit such behaviors and thoughts, we will be more receptive to the Holy Ghost and His whisperings.

As you get dressed and prepare yourself to attend the temple, it is worth looking in the mirror and asking yourself, "Is there anything about my appearance or dress that might be distracting to others or that might show an irreverence for the Lord and His sacred work?" Certain types of clothing, extreme hairstyles, or even having a few days of "scruff" on a young man's face *can* be inappropriate—contingent upon the circumstance. Thus, if you sense that there is anything about your appearance that you think *might* distract from the Spirit of worship and reverence that should prevail in the house of the Lord, change it—if you're able. This will help the Spirit of the Lord to be freely felt, and it will make it easier for others to focus on the ordinances being performed and the Spirit accompanying them.

Note

1. Robert L. Simpson, "Administration of Temples," in *Encyclopedia of Mormonism*, Daniel H. Ludlow, ed., four volumes (New York: Macmillan, 1994), 4:1457.

23

Why is the baptismal font in the temple traditionally resting on the backs of twelve oxen?

The baptismal fonts in the various temples of The Church of Jesus Christ of Latter-day Saints are patterned after the "molten sea" (or washing laver) in Solomon's temple, where the temple priests would purify themselves when they entered the sanctuary or temple. The book of 2 Chronicles describes the "molten sea" as follows:

> Also he made a molten sea . . . And under it was the similitude of oxen, which did compass it round about: . . . It stood upon twelve oxen, three looking toward the north, and three looking toward the west, and three looking toward the south, and three looking toward the east: and the sea was set above upon [the backs of] them, and all their hinder parts were [facing] inward. (2 Chronicles 4:2–4; see also 1 Kings 7:23–25)

This description well mirrors the fonts in our Latter-day Saint temples today.

But why do we place our temple baptismal fonts on the backs of twelve oxen? Why not use in the temple a plain rectangular font, like those at stake centers and churches throughout the world? Well, the symbolism is what's important here. The temple constantly uses symbols as teaching tools—and the baptismal font is no exception.

First of all, the number twelve is connected to two gospel ideas. It is associated with the priesthood (e.g., boys typically get ordained in their twelfth year, and there are twelve Apostles). Therefore, this reminds us that baptism must be done by proper priesthood authority if it is to be acceptable to God. Second, twelve is also the number associated with the tribes of Israel (i.e., the twelve tribes). Thus, symbolically speaking, baptism is the means by which you and I—and those for whom we perform vicarious baptisms—become one of the twelve tribes, or part of covenant Israel.

Why does the font rest on the backs of oxen? Oxen were used anciently as symbols of Christ and His disciples. Having the font on the backs of oxen, then, symbolizes who it is that supports the convert in his or her decision to be baptized. The symbolism suggests that Jesus and the members of the Church will support all those who enter into the baptismal covenant. It reminds you and me that we need to support each other—and particularly those who are weak or new in the faith. (Remember, part of what you promised at your own baptism was that you would be "willing to mourn with those that mourn; yea, and comfort those that stand in need of comfort"—Mosiah 18:9.)

Why are the oxen placed so that they face north, south, east, and west? There are four "cardinal" (or main) directions on the compass. Anciently, four was the number associated with geographic totality. In other words, in ancient times, if something faced all different directions, it symbolically implied that it was for *all* people or applied to *everyone.* Therefore, the oxen face every direction so as to symbolize the fact that *everyone* needs the ordinance of baptism if they hope to be saved in the celestial kingdom.

Baptismal fonts—including those in the temple—are traditionally placed below ground level. The reason for this is found in the words of the Apostle Paul, who taught that baptism is a symbol of our death, burial, and resurrection (Romans 6:3–5). Just as we go down in the water when we are baptized, a body goes down in the grave when the person dies—and graves are traditionally below ground level. In addition, just as we come up out of the water after we are baptized, in the resurrection we shall all rise up out of our graves, to a newness of life. Thus, the baptismal font is typically placed below ground level to symbolize that in being baptized, we are committing to let the old, sinful us die, and we are promising that we will come out of the water committed to a new, holy, and spiritual life. This is as much true for the deceased person who is accepting the baptism you perform for them in the temple as it was for you the day you were baptized a member of Christ's Church.

24

If there are baptisms for the dead, are there also confirmations for the dead?

Yes, both the ordinances of baptism and confirmation are necessary for salvation—not simply for the living, but also for the deceased.

Baptism offers the deceased the opportunity—if he or she accepts the vicarious ordinance—to have a covenant relationship with God and Christ. Confirmation makes it possible for the baptized person to be both sanctified (or cleansed of their sins) and also directed (or inspired) beyond his or her own natural capacity. Why, you might ask, would a deceased person need either of these things? Well, the deceased are as much alive as you and I are. Thus, in the spirit world they have the chance to accept the fullness of the gospel and to then become a missionary—sharing the gospel with other spirits who did not have a chance to hear and accept the gospel during mortality. In order to serve as an authorized missionary in the spirit world, one needs that covenant relationship with God (that comes through baptism), and one needs to be inspired as he or she teaches (which the gift of the Holy Ghost—given at confirmation—makes possible). So every deceased person who has a baptism for the dead performed vicariously on his or her behalf will *also* need to be confirmed a member of Christ's restored Church.

Usually, after a vicarious baptism has been performed, the deceased person's name is sent over to a confirmation room (in the temple) where someone will be confirmed a member of The Church of Jesus Christ of Latter-day Saints on their behalf. (While it is possible that you will perform both the baptism and the confirmation for a deceased individual, often one patron will perform the baptism and another will perform the confirmation for the same deceased person.)

The joy that being vicariously baptized and confirmed brings to the hearts of the deceased is something you and I cannot comprehend.

The Initiatory Ordinances

25

What are the initiatory ordinances?

The word *initiatory* comes from the root word *initiate* and means "beginning" or "to begin." Thus, the initiatory ordinances are the *beginning* of the higher ordinances of the temple, specifically the beginning of the endowment ceremony.[1] President Boyd K. Packer (1924–2015)—former President of the Quorum of the Twelve Apostles—explained, "The ordinances of washing and anointing are referred to often in the temple as *initiatory ordinances.*"[2] In the *Encyclopedia of Mormonism*, we are informed that in the temple there are "cubicles in which individuals are ritually washed and anointed before endowments can be performed."[3] Elsewhere we read, "Washings and anointings are preparatory or *initiatory* ordinances in the temple. They signify the cleansing and sanctifying power of Jesus Christ applied to the attributes of the person and to the hallowing of all life."[4] In section 124 of the Doctrine and Covenants, the Lord referred to these ordinances, stating, "Your anointings, and your washings . . . are ordained by the ordinance of my holy house" (D&C 124:39). "The initiatory ordinances are not only found in the modern Church, but they have biblical precedents."[5]

The *Encyclopedia of Mormonism* cites Exodus 28:41 as an example of a washing and anointing rite that took place in Old Testament times: "And thou shalt put them [i.e., the 'holy garments' or temple robes] upon Aaron thy brother, and his sons with him; and shalt anoint them, and consecrate them, and sanctify them, that they may minister unto me in the priest's office." Exodus 40:12–13 similarly states, "And thou shalt bring Aaron and his sons unto the door of the tabernacle of the congregation, and wash them with water.

And thou shalt put upon Aaron the holy garments, and anoint him, and sanctify him; that he may minister unto me in the priest's office."[6] We know that ritual washings like these were common in biblical times, but also in early Christianity.[7] One sixth-century Christian initiation ritual went like this:

> I sign [or anoint with oil in the sign of the cross] your forehead in the name of the Father, the Son and the Holy Spirit so that you may be a Christian. I sign [or anoint] your eyes so that they may see the glory of God. I sign your ears so that you may hear the voice of the Lord. I sign your nostrils so that you may breathe the fragrance of Christ. I sign your lips so that you may speak the words of life. I sign your heart so that you may believe in the Holy Trinity. I sign your shoulders so that you may bear the yoke of Christ's service. I sign your whole body, in the name of the Father and of the Son and of the Holy Ghost, so that you may live forever and ever.[8]

Latter-day Saint scholar Donald W. Parry explained:

> To ensure religious purity, Mosaic law required that designated individuals receive a ritual washing, sometimes in preparation for entering the temple (Ex. 30:17–21; Lev. 14:7–8; 15:5–27). . . .
>
> Many symbolic meanings of washings and anointings are traceable in the scriptures. Ritual washings (Heb. 9:10: D&C 124:37) symbolize the cleansing of the soul from sins and iniquities. They signify the washing-away of the pollutions of the Lord's people (Isa. 4:4). Psalm 51:2 expresses the human longing and divine promise: "Wash me thoroughly from mine iniquity, and cleanse me from my sin" (cf. Ps. 73:13; Isa. 1:16).
>
> The anointing of a person or object with sacred ointment [or oil] represents sanctification (Lev. 8:10–12) and consecration (Ex. 28:41), so that both become "most holy" (Ex. 30:29) unto the Lord. In this manner, profane persons and things are sanctified in similitude of the messiah (Hebrew "anointed one"), who is Christ (Greek "anointed one").[9]

As suggested, in ancient times, washing with water was often seen as a symbol of the cleansing of a person, making him or her free from sin. Anointing with oil, on the other hand, usually carried the connotation of the Holy Spirit being poured out upon the anointed one, that they might be inspired by God—that they might be a recipient of personal revelation. As in ancient times, the initiatory ordinances today prepare Latter-day Saints to receive the full blessings of the temple. They prepare the initiate to receive his or her ordinances in a state of cleanliness before the Lord. They prepare the initiate for the inspiration available through the holy endowment, and they introduce those being endowed to the symbolic way in which temple truths are conveyed.

Notes

1. See Allen Claire Rozsa, "Temple Ordinances," in *Encyclopedia of Mormonism*, Daniel H. Ludlow, ed., four volumes (New York: Macmillan, 1994), 1:444; Ed J. Pinegar, *The Temple: Gaining Knowledge and Power in the House of the Lord* (American Fork, UT: Covenant Communications, 2014), 121–122.

2. Boyd K. Packer, *The Holy Temple* (Salt Lake City, UT: Bookcraft, 1980), 154, emphasis added.

3. Immo Luschin, "Latter-day Saint Temple Worship and Activity," in *Encyclopedia of Mormonism*, Daniel H. Ludlow, ed., four volumes (New York: Macmillan, 1994), 4:1447. See also "Q&A: Questions and Answers," in *New Era* (January 1994), 17. Hugh Nibley wrote, "First, there is an initiatory stage in which one is physically set apart from the world: actually washed, anointed, given a protective garment, and clothed in sanctified robes. This is merely preliminary and qualifies one to proceed, in earnest not of what one has become, but of what one may and wishes to become." Hugh Nibley, *Approaching Zion* (Provo/Salt Lake City, UT: Foundation for Ancient Research and Mormon Studies/Deseret Book, 1989), 424.

4. See "anoint" and "washing," in Andrew H. Hedges et al., eds., *Journals, Volume 3: May 1843–June 1844*, vol. 3 of the Journals series of *The Joseph Smith Papers*, ed. Ronald K. Esplin and Matthew J. Grow (Salt Lake City: Church Historian's Press, 2015), 478 & 490.

5. Allen Claire Rozsa, "Temple Ordinances," in *Encyclopedia of Mormonism*, Daniel H. Ludlow, ed., four volumes (New York: Macmillan, 1994), 4:1444.

6. See Frank W. Hirschi, "Consecration," in *Encyclopedia of Mormonism*, Daniel H. Ludlow, ed., four volumes (New York: Macmillan, 1994), 1:312.

7. See Allen Claire Rozsa, "Temple Ordinances," in *Encyclopedia of Mormonism*, Daniel H. Ludlow, ed., four volumes (New York: Macmillan, 1994), 1:444; Donald W. Parry, "Washings and Anointings," in *Encyclopedia of Mormonism*, Daniel H. Ludlow, ed., four volumes (New York: Macmillan, 1994), 4:1551.

8. See Arthur McCormack, *Christian Initiation* (New York: Hawthorn Publishers, 1969), 50.

9. Donald W. Parry, "Washings and Anointings," in *Encyclopedia of Mormonism*, Daniel H. Ludlow, ed., four volumes (New York: Macmillan, 1994), 4:1551.

26

Are the initiatory ordinances part of the endowment, or are they a totally separate ordinance?

While the initiatory ordinances are performed in a different part of the temple than is the remainder of the endowment, as mentioned earlier (see Question #25), formally speaking, the initiatory is the "beginning" of the endowment—as the name *initiatory* suggests.

The reason they are performed in different parts of the temple is solely practical. The initiatory involves the use of water and oil and also changing (in a locker room) into the clothing you'll be wearing during the remainder of the endowment. Thus, for the purposes of privacy and convenience, they are performed in different parts of the temple. Nevertheless, they are all part of your temple endowment.

27

How can I best prepare for what I will experience during the temple initiatory ordinances?

Thinking about the various questions and their answers in this section of the book will help you to be better prepared for what you will experience when you participate in the initiatory ordinances of the temple. Yet there is more that you can do.

Because what happens in the temple—including in the initiatory ordinances—is highly symbolic, thinking a bit about symbols *before* you go to the temple may help you to better understand what is happening once you are there.

Anciently, each part of the body had a symbolic meaning attached to it. Therefore, in various ancient rituals, parts of the body were emphasized in order to send a symbolic message to the person who was being initiated. For example:

+ Eyes are often symbolic of what one chooses to view or observe.
+ Ears are commonly symbolic of what one chooses to listen to or obey.
+ The nose was an ancient symbol for the need to control one's temper.
+ The mouth can symbolize the things one chooses to speak.
+ Arms and hands were often a symbol for what one chooses to do.
+ Legs and feet commonly symbolized the path one chooses to pursue.
+ The heart or breast was an ancient symbol for what one allowed oneself to love.

♦ The brain traditionally represented one's thoughts—both good and evil.

Thinking about such things before and during your initiatory ordinances will help you to have a better sense of what the Lord is trying to teach you.

As noted previously (see Question #25), water was a common symbol in ancient times for the Holy Ghost's ability to sanctify or cleanse you. It is for this reason that we use water when one is baptized, as it reminds us that the person who has been immersed is now clean before the Lord.

Olive oil was used in ancient times as a symbol for the Spirit's power to inspire or give revelation—in addition to its power to protect. Thus, prophets, priests, and kings were anointed with oil in the hope that they would be instruments of the Holy Spirit, inspired, directed, and protected in their sacred work. Latter-day Saint scholar Hugh Nibley (1910–2005) wrote, "The anointing of the brow, face, ears, nose, breast, etc., represents 'the clothing of the [anointed person] in the protective panoply of the Holy Spirit.'"[1]

Horns were commonly used in the Old Testament because they were symbols for power. Thus, if an altar had horns on its corners (as ancient altars often did), it represented the power of the sacrifice being made on the altar (Exodus 29:12). If a horn was used to hold olive oil, it symbolized the power of the anointing that one was receiving—or the power being offered to the one being anointed (1 Samuel 16:13).

The laying on of hands was an ancient symbol of the conveyance or transfer of power. One in authority would lay his hands upon the person being blessed to imply that he was placing upon the person being blessed things like power, authority, or great blessings—all of which stem from God.

One scholar pointed out: "In the Book of Mormon and Doctrine and Covenants, *anointing* is often associated with royal anointing (Ether 9:4; Doctrine and Covenants 109:80)."[2] Both anciently and today, kings and queens are typically seated when they are anointed, and being seated represents enthronement, or the right to preside over one's nation, posterity, or creations.

There are many symbols that you will notice during the initiatory ordinances. As you pay attention to them and ponder them, the Spirit can whisper to you sacred meanings and implications of what you are being promised through those holy ordinances.

Notes

1. Hugh Nibley, "Meanings and Functions of Temples," in *Encyclopedia of Mormonism*, Daniel H. Ludlow, ed., four volumes (New York: Macmillan, 1992), 4:1461.
2. Thomas A. Wayment, *The New Testament: A Translation for Latter-day Saints* (Provo, UT: Brigham Young University Religious Studies Center, 2019), 125.

28

What do I need to take with me to the temple when I receive my initiatory ordinances and my endowment?

When you receive your initiatory ordinances and your endowment in the temple, you will need to take with you several things.

First of all, if you're able, take with you someone you are close to, someone who is the same gender as you (who has already received his or her own endowment) and who can serve as your escort in the temple that day (see Question #36). If you don't have anyone, the ordinance workers at the temple will ask someone to escort you.

Second, you will need to bring with you your temple recommend and also a recommend for living ordinances (see Question #11). Your bishop will issue those to you, and both your bishop and stake president will sign them for you. Because you will need an interview with both your bishop (or branch president) and stake (or mission) president to get these two recommends, you'll want to set appointments for those interviews several weeks before you plan on receiving your endowment.

Third, you will need to take with you to your initiatory/ endowment a pair of new temple garments. You should leave those unopened in the package in which they came. If you do not have a family member who can help you select a pair of temple garments, your bishop or Relief Society president would be happy to help you pick which style of temple garments you might be most comfortable wearing. (There are many different styles and fabrics.)

Fourth, special clothing is worn in the temple by those participating in the sacred ordinances (see Question #43). Some temples will have clothing you can rent. However, others may not. If the temple you will receive your initiatory/endowment in does not have a clothing rental, you may need to bring your own temple clothes. Well before the day of your endowment, call the temple you plan on receiving your ordinances in and ask them if they have clothing rental services. If they do not, an endowed family member or your bishop or Relief Society president can help you to get the clothing you will need for that special day.

29

Why do those who have received their initiatory ordinances wear temple garments afterward?

Many ancient and modern religions have sacred underclothing as part of their tradition. Ancient Jewish priests (who worked in the tabernacle) had a special shirt (Exodus 28:39) and linen underpants (Exodus 28:42) that they wore as part of their temple service. Modern Orthodox Jews also have a sacred undershirt that they wear daily, as do practitioners of Zoroastrianism (a Persian faith traced back to Zarathustra). Members of the Sikh faith (a religion based out of the Punjab region of India, which began in the fifteenth century) wear special underpants that remind them of the importance of living the commandments of their faith. Even some Eastern Orthodox Christians wear a cloth *phylakton* on their undergarments as a "protection against evil."[1]

The temple garment Latter-day Saints receive when they participate in the initiatory ordinances is a symbol of the covenants they have entered into in the house of the Lord.[2] "The garment, covering the body, is a visual and tactile reminder of those covenants. For many Church members the garment has formed a barrier of protection when the wearer has been faced with temptations. Among other things, [the garment] symbolizes our deep respect for the laws of God—among them the moral standard."[3] While the garment is only made of cloth—and cloth is *not*, in and of itself, sacred—nevertheless, what it symbolizes is sacred. For that reason, we treat the garment with reverence. The garment is worn throughout the life of the temple-endowed Latter-day Saint as a constant reminder of the covenants he or she has made. The *Encyclopedia of Mormonism* explains, "Garments bear several simple marks of orientation toward the gospel principles of obedience, truth, life, and discipleship in Christ."[4] If the wearer symbolically attaches to the garment these meanings, then the temple garment can function as a "shield and a protection" against temptation and sin.[5] Attaching meaning to the garment can help the wearer remember his or her covenants and to trust that Christ will cover his or her sins. Some have claimed miraculous physical protection from injury and harm because of the garment. While I do not call into question such miracles, it is important to realize that the primary promise of protection associated with the garment has to do with temptation and sin, and not the miraculous preservation of the mortal life—for all must ultimately die in order to return to God's presence.

Another reason for wearing the garment each day has to do with its connections with Christ. The Hebrew word for *atonement* means quite literally to "cover." Just as Jesus's Atonement covers our sins, the garment covers our nakedness—which is itself a symbol for sin. Because the temple garment is sometimes associated with the "flesh of Christ" (Hebrews 10:20), it seems an appropriate symbol for Christ's Atonement on our behalf. It reminds us each and every day that Jesus is willing to cover our sins *if* we strive to live in harmony with His commandments and the covenants we have made (John 14:6).

Finally, the temple garment is associated with the garments worn by the ancient temple priests (see Question #43). Thus, it can remind us of our call to do God's work every day. We are to be on His errand. We are to be instruments in His hands every day of our lives.

If we symbolically attach such meanings to our temple garments, they will help us throughout our lives to more fully keep our covenants, to more meaningfully serve others, to more fully trust in God's grace and mercy, and to more completely develop Jesus's attributes and nature; thereby qualifying us to return to God's presence and dwell with Him for eternity.[6]

Notes

1. For a detailed discussion of each of these articles of "sacred underwear" and their symbolic meaning, see Alonzo L. Gaskill, "'Clothed upon with Glory': Sacred Underwear and the Consecrated Life," in *Temple Reflections: Insights into the House of the Lord* (Springville, UT: Cedar Fort, 2016), 36–54.

2. Evelyn T. Marshall, "Garments," in *Encyclopedia of Mormonism*, Daniel H. Ludlow, ed., four volumes (New York: Macmillan, 1992), 2:534. See also Carlos E. Asay, "The Temple Garment: An Outward Expression of an Inward Commitment," in *Ensign*, August 1997, 19; Ed J. Pinegar, *The Temple: Gaining Knowledge and Power in the House of the Lord* (American Fork, UT: Covenant Communications, 2014), 89.

3. Boyd K. Packer, *The Holy Temple* (Salt Lake City, UT: Bookcraft, 1980), 79. See also J. Richard Clark, "The Temple—What It Means to You," in *New Era*, April 1993, 4.

4. Evelyn T. Marshall, "Garments," in in *Encyclopedia of Mormonism*, Daniel H. Ludlow, ed., four volumes (New York: Macmillan, 1992), 2:534.

5. Boyd K. Packer, *The Holy Temple* (Salt Lake City, UT: Bookcraft, 1980), 265; Erastus Snow, discourse given March 3, 1878, in *Journal of Discourses* 19:272.

6. The Church has produced a helpful video, titled "Sacred Temple Clothing," which talks about the temple garment. You can find this in the Media Library on lds.org. You may wish to watch this video prior to receiving your endowment, or as an aid in explaining to others why Latter-day Saints wear temple garments.

30

Where do I purchase temple garments?

In many parts of the world, the Church has Distribution Services Stores (often referred to as "distribution centers"), which sell temple garments and other clothing worn in the temple. Your bishop, Relief Society president, or an endowed member of your ward or family will know if there is one near where you live.

If you happen to live in a part of the world where there is no Church distribution center, it is possible to order temple garments (and other temple clothing) online at www.store.lds.org.

If you have to order your temple clothing through the internet, make certain that you order what you need well in advance of the day that you will be receiving your endowment, just to ensure that they arrive in time for your special day.

In addition, if you have to order your garments and temple clothing online, it will be helpful to have a person who has already received their endowment sitting alongside you as you place your order. That way, you will be sure to get everything you need. (If you purchase your temple clothing at a Church distribution center, the employees can help ensure that you have everything you need.)

31

I've heard that in the temple someone "washes" you. Is that really true?

I remember hearing this myself prior to receiving my temple endowment, and I recall being a bit concerned. It turns out, this is not really accurate—at least not in the sense that we typically use the term "wash."

In Question #25, we talked about what the initiatory ordinances are. There we highlighted some of what you can expect when you participate in this ordinance.

The "washing" that is part of the initiatory ordinance is a representative act, not an actual *washing* in the sense that the word typically implies.[1] It is a symbolic gesture. While it is only a small symbolic action, it represents a much greater truth, namely, that you and I need Christ's Atonement to cleanse us completely—from head to toe. We can sin in so many ways—in what we think, in what we view, in what we listen to, in what we say, and so on. The figurative "washing" you have heard about reminds us of Christ's power to cleanse us from *all* of our sins, no matter how we committed them or with which part of our body we sinned (e.g., thinking bad thoughts, speaking unkind words, pursuing unholy paths, etc.).

Note

1. See Alvin R. Dyer, *For What Purpose?* (Independence, MO: Central States Mission, 1962), 8; Oliver Cowdery Diary, 21 January 1836, cited in *The Papers of Joseph Smith*, volume 2, Dean C. Jessee, ed. (Salt Lake City, UT: Deseret Book, 1992), 159, note 1.

32

I've heard that in the temple you get a "new name." What is that about?

When you were born, your parents selected a name for you, the name by which you would be known throughout your life. Some of us get a nickname that sticks, and it becomes a new name by which we are commonly known. When she gets married, a woman might take her husband's last name as a way of saying the two of them are united. King Benjamin gave his people a new name (Mosiah 5:7–14) because they had entered into a covenant to "take upon [themselves] the name of Christ" (v. 10). The practice of giving "new names" to people when participating in an ordinance can be traced back to the earliest of times. One source states, "The giving or possessing of a second name, to be kept hidden from others, is widely attested in antiquity."[1]

In the Church, one potentially receives a "new name" at birth (when one's parents choose a name for the newborn), at baptism (when one receives the name of "Christian"), upon ordination (when one now holds a titled priesthood office), when making certain covenants (such as in the temple[2]), and, in some cases, when married (if a woman chooses to take upon herself her husband's last name). Each of these events signals a new stage in one's life, as does the accompanying name. One dictionary of scriptural names indicates that each "new name" has meaning, so much so that sometimes, when a person's nature changed, God changed his or her name also.[3] For example, Abram's name was changed to Abraham, Simon's was changed to Cephas/Peter, and Saul's name was changed to Paul. "If naming constituted the giving of an identity, the giving of a new name gave a new identity to the recipient, and was frequently associated with an important transition in the recipient's life."[4]

> Taking upon oneself a new name is a symbol of becoming a
> new person. . . . The new name is a token [or symbol that one]
> has been spiritually reborn, that his "old man is crucified with
> [Christ]," as Paul would say (Romans 6:6), and that he has over
> time become a new person. This sanctification journey . . . is
> the same journey of renewal described by King Benjamin . . . in
> chapters 2 through 4 of the book of Mosiah. . . . It teaches
> unequivocally that salvation can come to none except those who
> will repent and accept Christ as their savior, take upon themselves
> His name, and become new people—be born again—through
> His Atonement (see Mosiah 3:17; 5:8). . . . Benjamin insists that
> accepting Christ's salvation means undergoing a change of heart
> and character.[5]

In the book of Revelation, Jesus tells us that those who enter the celestial kingdom will receive "a white stone, and in the stone a new name [will be] written, which [name] no man knoweth saving he that receiveth it" (Revelation 2:17). Doctrine and Covenants section 130 makes a similar promise, but adds an additional detail: "And a white stone[6] is given to each of those who come into the celestial kingdom, whereon is a new name written, which no man knoweth save he that receiveth it. *The new name is the key word*" (D&C 130:11, emphasis added). Of this "new name," and its function as a "key word," ancient tradition held that possession of the "'white stone' . . . could, by use of the name written on it, 'secure entrance into heaven.'" It gave one power to part the veil that separated God and man, and it allowed the possessor of the new name to return to God's presence—endowing the holder with "supernatural powers."[7]

Now, some have assumed that the new name received in the temple was their heavenly name, the name by which they were called in the premortal world, or the name by which they will be called in the eternities. However, the ordinances of the temple do not make that claim, nor have the prophets—ancient or modern. Rather, the new name functions as a "key"—a symbol, *per se.*

President Joseph Fielding Smith (1876–1972), tenth President of the Church, elaborated on this idea.

The ordinances of the temple, the endowment and sealings, pertain to exaltation in the celestial kingdom, where the sons and daughters are. The sons and daughters [of God] are not outside in some other kingdom. The sons and daughters go into the house, belong to the household, have access to the home. "In my Father's house are many mansions." Sons and daughters have access to the home where he dwells, and you cannot receive that access until you go to the temple. Why? Because you must receive certain key words as well as make covenants by which you are able to enter. If you try to get into the house, and the door is locked, how are you going to enter, if you haven't your key? You get your key in the temple, which will admit you.

I picked up a key on the street one day, and took it home, and it opened every door in my house. [In those days, keys were pretty universal, and opened most locks.] You cannot find a key on the street . . . that will open the door that enters into our Father's mansions. You have got to go where the key is given. And each can obtain the key, if you will; but after receiving it, you may lose it, by having it taken away from you again, unless you abide by the agreement which you entered into when you went to the house of the Lord.[8]

The concept of a new name suggests that one has access to God, and that one will have the "key" necessary to enter into God's kingdom if he or she lives a life of faithfulness to his or her covenants—and to God's commandments. Receiving a new name implies a transition, a new identity. The recipient has died to sin, and has been "born again" into a newness of life—the type of life that will allow him or her to dwell with God for eternity.

Notes

1. Bruce H. Porter and Stephen D. Ricks, "Names in Antiquity: Old, New, and Hidden," in John M. Lundquist and Stephen D. Ricks, ed. *By Study and Also By Faith*, two volumes (Provo, UT: Foundation for Ancient Research and Mormon Studies, 1990), 1:508.

2. See Susan Easton Black, "I Have a Question," in *Ensign*, December 1988, 54–55; Charles C. Rich, discourse given February 10, 1878, in *Journal of Discourses* 19:250; Alvin R. Dyer, *For What Purpose?* (Independence, MO: Central States Mission, 1962), 8; Ed J. Pinegar, *The Temple: Gaining Knowledge and Power in the House of the Lord* (American Fork, UT: Covenant Communications, 2014), 124; John W. Welch, in Hugh Nibley, *Teachings of the Book of Mormon—Part Four* (Provo, UT: Foundations for Ancient Research and Mormon Studies, 2004), 161-162; Hugh Nibley, *The Message of the Joseph Smith Papyri: An Egyptian Endowment*, second edition (Provo, UT: Foundation for Ancient Research and Mormon Studies, 2005), 190, 527.

3. See Judson Cornwall and Stelman Smith, *The Exhaustive Dictionary of Bible Names* (North Brunswick, New Jersey: Bridge-Logos Publishers, 1998), vii.

4. Bruce H. Porter and Stephen D. Ricks, "Names in Antiquity: Old, New, and Hidden," in John M. Lundquist and Stephen D. Ricks, ed. *By Study and Also By Faith*, two volumes (Provo, UT: Foundation for Ancient Research and Mormon Studies, 1990), 1:513.

5. Gerald E. Hansen Jr., *Sacred Walls: Learning from Temple Symbolism* (American Fork, UT: Covenant Communications, 2009), 43.

6. The "white stone" will act as a Urim and Thummim to all who receive it, whereby—as Gods—they may know all things pertaining to any kingdom, past, present, or future. See D&C 130:9–10.

7. See Joseph Fielding McConkie and Craig J. Ostler, *Revelations of the Restorations* (Salt Lake City, UT: Deseret Book, 2000), 1048.

8. Joseph Fielding Smith, *Doctrines of Salvation*, three volumes in one, Bruce R. McConkie, compiler (Salt Lake City, UT: Bookcraft, 1998), 2:40–41, emphasis in original.

33

Is it true that women perform the initiatory ordinances for women and men perform them for men?

Yes, in the temple, women are set apart to perform the introductory portion of the endowment for women, and men for men (see Question #31).[1] President Dallin H. Oaks (b. 1932) of the First Presidency recently taught that this "sacred work that sisters do in the temple" is "under the keys held by the temple president."[2] Emma Smith (1804–1879), the Prophet Joseph's wife, was the first woman in this dispensation to receive the temple endowment, including the washing and anointing. After she received her own endowment, she began performing the initiatory ordinances for other women.[3]

Though we do not know much about our Mother in Heaven, through modern revelation, we know that She exists and that She is an integral part of the great plan of happiness.[4] President Spencer W. Kimball (1895–1985), twelfth President of the Church, taught, "When we sing that doctrinal hymn and anthem of affection, 'O My Father,' we get a sense of the ultimate in maternal modesty, of the restrained, queenly elegance of our heavenly mother, and knowing how profoundly our mortal mothers have shaped us here, do we suppose her influence on us as individuals to be less if we live so as to return there?"[5] Just as men represent Heavenly Father and Jesus when they function in the temple, surely in the initiatory ordinances for women, one catches a possible glimpse of what Mother in Heaven must be like as She works on behalf of Her children here upon the earth. For sisters in the Church, one of the choicest experiences had in the temple is often during the initiatory ordinances, where women perform these most sacred ordinances on behalf of other women.

Notes

1. Allen Claire Rozsa, "Temple Ordinances," in *Encyclopedia of Mormonism*, Daniel H. Ludlow, ed., four volumes (New York: Macmillan, 1994), 4:1444.
2. Dallin H. Oaks, "The Keys and Authority of the Priesthood," in *Ensign*, May 2014, 50.
3. Joseph Smith, Journal, Sept. 28, 1843, in Andrew H. Hedges et al., eds., *Journals, Volume 3: May 1843–June 1844,* vol. 3 of the Journals series of *The Joseph Smith Papers*, ed. Ronald K. Esplin and Matthew J. Grow (Salt Lake City: Church Historian's Press, 2015), 104. See notes 481 & 483.
4. See, for example, "Mother in Heaven" Gospel Topics Essay, https://www.lds. org/topics/mother-in-heaven?lang=eng; Elaine Cannon, "Mother in Heaven," in *Encyclopedia of Mormonism*, Daniel H. Ludlow, ed., four volumes (New York: Macmillan, 1994), 2:961; David L. Paulsen and Martin Pulido, "'A Mother There': A Survey of Historical Teachings about Mother in Heaven," *BYU Studies*, 50, no. 1 (2011), 70–97.
5. Spencer W. Kimball, *The Teachings of Spencer W. Kimball* (Salt Lake City, UT: Bookcraft, 1998), 327.

𝟥𝟦

Do you have a family member or friend with you when you receive your initiatory ordinances?

On the day that you receive your endowment in the temple, you will either take with you an endowed family member or friend to act as your escort, or the temple will assign someone to serve in that capacity for you (see Question #36). That first day in the temple, you will constantly have help nearby, just in case you have a question or need direction. Indeed, *each time* you enter the temple, there are ordinance workers stationed everywhere, just in case someone needs assistance. Such is the case when you receive your initiatory ordinances also.

The Endowment

35

What does the word "endowment" mean?

The word *endowment* is traditionally understood to mean a "gift," "bequest," "inheritance," or "legacy." A financial or monetary endowment—such as might be established at a university—is a gift consisting of a significant amount of money that gives its recipient power (through the newly received wealth) and also a longevity of blessings (as such endowments are traditionally set up so as to ensure the recipient will have perpetual income off of the interest of the gift).

In like manner, the temple endowment is a gift from God. It promises those who receive it (through making and keeping sacred covenants) significant spiritual blessings, including "power from on high" and other perpetual gifts that, so long as we are faithful, will never stop blessing us.

One of the greatest gifts God offers us through the holy endowment is fuller access to and greater knowledge of Christ's Atonement—including all of the gifts derived therefrom. As we live the covenants we make in the holy temple, gifts of power, protection, and spiritual insight can flow into our lives. As we frequently and prayerfully attend the temple, we will feel more sanctified, clean, holy, and equipped to face the challenges of life.

Sometimes you will hear members of the Church say, "I am going to *take out* my endowment." It may be better to say "receive" rather than "take out." The endowment is a gift from God. It is not truly our place to "take" that gift. Rather, we go to the temple to "receive" the gifts God desires to give to us, contingent upon our faithfulness.

36

What is a temple endowment "escort"?

A temple "escort" is someone of your same gender who has already received his or her endowment, holds a current temple recommend, and can be with you on the day you receive your temple endowment. He or she will be by your side to help you as you participate in the various ordinances of the temple. Your escort can answer questions for you and help you to know where to go and what to do. They will even help you to know how to put on your temple robes (see Question #44). The point of having an escort with you is to limit the stress you may feel—since everything is so new to you.

Ideally, select someone you are close to and whom you get along well with. This will make your day more special and less stressful.

{ 37 }

How old do I need to be in order
to receive my endowment?

There isn't an established age at which one can receive his or her endowment, though most will be *at least* eighteen years of age. (A man *must* hold the Melchizedek Priesthood in order to receive his endowment, and that usually only happens *after* he is at least eighteen years of age.) Rather than focusing on the age of the applicant, the bishop and stake president seek instead to determine the candidate's spiritual and emotional maturity, personal preparation and conduct, and reason for seeking to enter the temple. Things such as the depth of one's testimony or gospel understanding are certainly factors in determining whether one is ready to enter the house of the Lord and make sacred covenants. How one answers the temple recommend questions also plays a role. In some circumstances, the degree to which one has been faithful in his or her previous Church service may suggest his or her level of commitment to covenants. Thus, there are many factors in determining when one is ready to receive his or her endowment, though the specific age of the candidate is not the primary determinant (see Question # 9).

38

Do I need to be going on a mission or be engaged in order to receive my endowment?

Though in times past, many who received their endowment were either waiting to enter the mission field or waiting to be sealed to a spouse, the current policy does not require that one be pursuing a mission or a marriage in order to receive his or her endowment.

That being said, there are good reasons and bad reasons for wanting to receive one's endowment. Having a mission call or being engaged to be married are good reasons to seek to make sacred covenants with God. Wanting to be in attendance at a roommate, friend, or family member's sealing is not a great reason to make these higher covenants. Our primary purpose for receiving our endowment should be our desire to make covenants with our Father in Heaven. While there is nothing inappropriate about wanting to see a friend or family member sealed, the covenants taken in the temple are too sacred to be casually entered into for the ulterior purpose of witnessing a marriage ceremony. If making sacred covenants is a secondary reason for receiving one's endowment, and some other goal is the primary reason, it would be inappropriate to seek to receive one's temple endowment.

39

Why would a person receive his or her endowment before going on a mission or before being sealed to a spouse?

Most missions are hard, and many marriages are too. On your mission, you may have challenges with your companions, difficulties finding people to teach, members who are unsupportive, and temptations that are overwhelming. Marriage and family life will also have its challenges. Personalities sometimes don't mesh, children sometimes don't obey, challenges sometimes arise, and the best of marriages require work. Both missions and marriages need constant revelation if they are to go as God intends. President Russell M. Nelson (b. 1924), seventeenth President of the Church, explained that "a temple marriage is not only between husband and wife; it also embraces a partnership with God (Matthew 19:6)."[1] Like a married couple, missionaries also need God's partnership, power, and protection (D&C 109:22, 25–26, 28). We would be foolish to embark on a marriage—or a mission—without God as our partner. With Father in Heaven at our side, we have our best chance of success. Your endowment makes that partnership possible. The purpose of the temple endowment is to enter you into a covenant relationship with God that, if you are faithful to the promises you make, will bring into your life power—power to avoid temptation, power to receive revelation, power to minister to others, power to navigate difficulties, and power to endure all things. Indeed, the Lord has said that "in the ordinances" of the temple, "the power of godliness is manifest" (D&C 84:20; see vv. 19–22). That "power of godliness" is desperately needed by each of us—on our missions and in our marriages. Having it will heal and help in all that we do.

President Nelson has also said, "Each temple ordinance is not just a ritual to go through; it is an act of solemn promising."[2] Your endowment is not "magic." The power doesn't come just because you went to the temple. It comes as you think about your covenants, live the commandments, and submit your will to God's. However, if you do those things—and do them consistently—you will find that Satan will have less influence in your life. You will see that you are less ruffled by challenges that come your way. You will find that your mission and your marriage will go better, and you will love more deeply those who become your companions (on your mission *and* in your marriage). God wants us to have our endowment before leaving for a mission or getting married because He knows we will have a much greater chance of succeeding *and enjoying* the journey with that spiritual power deeply rooted in our souls.

Notes

1. Russell M. Nelson, *Hope in Our Hearts* (Salt Lake City, UT: Deseret Book, 2009), 36.
2. Russell M. Nelson, *Hope in Our Hearts* (Salt Lake City, UT: Deseret Book, 2009), 103.

40

What does "born in the covenant" mean?

The phrase *born in the covenant* (or BIC, as it is commonly abbreviated) simply means that an infant was born to parents who were sealed to each other in the temple *prior to* the infant's birth.

One of the consequences of being born in the covenant is that the child, after being born, does not need to go to the temple to be sealed to his or her parents. By virtue of the parents' sealing before the child's birth, the child is born already sealed to his or her mother and father—and is already an heir to certain blessings associated with his or her parents' temple sealing. President Joseph Fielding Smith explained a few of those blessings that the child who is born in the covenant would be entitled to. He suggested that, by virtue of their sealing to their parents, they would have access to a greater measure of guidance than was generally available to the world, additional protection from sin and Satan, and increased access to inspiration from the Holy Spirit.[1]

President Boyd K. Packer (1924–2015)—former President of the Quorum of the Twelve Apostles—explained, "The sealing ordinance is that ordinance which binds families eternally. . . . When a couple is sealed in the temple *following* a civil marriage, the children born to them previous to that time, and therefore not born in the covenant, are sealed to them in a brief and sacred ordinance."[2] For those *not* born in the covenant but sealed to their parents later, once that sealing has been performed, it is as though the child *were* born in the covenant, and all those blessings associated with being born in the covenant would now be theirs.

Notes

1. See Joseph Fielding Smith, *Doctrines of Salvation*, three volumes in one, Bruce R. McConkie, complier (Salt Lake City, UT: Bookcraft, 1998), 2:90.
2. Boyd K. Packer, *The Holy Temple* (Salt Lake City, UT: Bookcraft, 1980), 155, emphasis added.

41

Who can or should be present when I receive my endowment?

Any worthy member of the Church who has already received his or her own endowment and who has a current temple recommend may attend the temple with you on the day you receive your endowment. In addition, if you have a friend or relative who chooses to receive his or her endowment in the same temple, on the same day, and at the same time as you, he or she too can be present for your endowment. (My best friend and I received our endowments together in the Salt Lake Temple.)

Because of the sacred nature of what you will be doing in the temple that day, and because of the reverence that should be present in the house of the Lord, it is best to not invite too large of a group to be in attendance when you receive your endowment. Sometimes individuals will invite their entire extended family or large groups from their ward to be in attendance. While it is appropriate to want to have those whom you love with you on this sacred day, it is important to remember that having too many people present can cause a celebratory or irreverent atmosphere. Because you will be attending the temple regularly the rest of your life, there is no need to have an exceedingly large group with you on the day you receive your endowment. You will have literally hundreds of opportunities to be in the temple with various family members and friends over the course of your lifetime.

42

How can I best prepare for what I will experience when I receive my temple endowment?

There are a number of things you can do to help you to be more prepared for the day when you will receive your holy endowment.

President Russell M. Nelson (b. 1924), seventeenth President of the Church, once counseled members of the Church preparing to receive their endowment, "Spiritual preparation is enhanced by study. I like to recommend that members going to the temple for the first time read short explanatory paragraphs in the Bible Dictionary, listed under seven topics: 'Anoint,' 'Atonement,' 'Christ,' 'Covenant,' 'Fall of Adam,' 'Sacrifices,' and 'Temple.' Doing so will provide a firm foundation."[1]

Taking a temple preparation course is also a good idea. While by design that course is largely focused on the doctrine behind temple work, nevertheless, it will help you to think more deeply about the sacred nature of what you are about to do.

There is value in reverently talking about the temple (and what you will experience therein) with individuals whom you are close to, who have received their own endowment, and who attend the temple regularly. They will have insights and thoughts that may serve to prepare you for your endowment.

In anticipation of receiving your own endowment, it may be helpful for you to spend some time doing family history work, and preparing/submitting to the temple the names of individuals who need their temple work done for them. This will certainly help you to catch the spirit of temple work, and may enable you to feel the thinness of the veil and the closeness of those who are seeking their ordinances from the spirit world.

If you live reasonably close to a temple, in the years, months, or weeks leading up to receiving your endowment, you should try to attend the Lord's house as often as you are able in order to participate in baptisms and confirmations for the dead. Those sacred ordinances are also part of temple work, and they are absolutely necessary for the redemption of the dead. The spirit that you will feel when you engage in baptisms for the dead will prepare you for the experience you will have when receiving your own endowment.

While it can be challenging, it may be helpful for you to practice thinking symbolically. Read a book or two on symbolism, as these will put your mind in "symbolism mode"—which will help you on the day of your endowment. Indeed, when you enter the temple to receive your endowment, it may be helpful to pick a thing or two to look for. For example, one Church publication suggested "everything in the temple points to the Savior."[2] So practice looking for things that remind you of Christ in your everyday world. Then, when you receive your endowment, look for things there that remind you of Jesus. That will help you to get more out of your first experience.

Perhaps the most important thing you can do in preparation to enter the house of the Lord is keep your life worthy and clean so that you will be receptive to the Spirit during your temple endowment. President Russell M. Nelson once noted, "We cannot cut corners of preparation and risk the breaking of covenants we were not prepared to make."[3] If you are not living a clean and spiritual life, you likely will not have a positive experience when you enter the temple because the Spirit—who testifies of truth—will be grieved and, thus, will not bear witness to your soul of the rightness of the things you are experiencing. If there are things that are amiss in your life, visit with your bishop and resolve those before you enter the holy temple (see Question #13).

Notes

1. Russell M. Nelson, *Hope in Our Hearts* (Salt Lake City, UT: Deseret Book, 2009), 106.
2. "Prepare for the Temple: Make Your Experience More Personal and Meaningful," https://www.lds.org/temples/prepare-for-your-temple-visit?lang=eng.
3. Russell M. Nelson, *Hope in Our Hearts* (Salt Lake City, UT: Deseret Book, 2009), 102.

43

Is there special clothing worn in the temple that isn't worn outside of the temple?

In Questions 29 and 30, we discussed the temple garment, which is worn throughout the lives of those who have made sacred covenants in the temple. In addition to the temple garment, there are other "sacred vestments" worn by Latter-day Saints known as "the robes of the Holy Priesthood."[1] One Latter-day Saint author explained, "In the stillness of the temple, we wear white pants and dresses, white robes and sashes, white caps and veils"[2] (see Exodus 28:4[3]). These vestments are only worn in the temple, or by a deceased Latter-day Saint at his or her funeral. (The Church has released a video—which is posted on LDS.org—and is titled "Sacred Temple Clothing." This short film shows the various articles of clothing worn in the temple. You may wish to watch this video *prior* to receiving your temple endowment.)

The idea of sacred vestments or special religious clothing was common anciently, as it is today. The priests of the Old Testament tabernacle and temple wore sacred vestments, which were highly symbolic. Today, Orthodox Jews traditionally wear a special head covering and also an undershirt and/or prayer shawl, each reminding them of what it means to be one of God's chosen people. Nuns and priests in the Roman Catholic tradition have special clothing they wear, which is symbolic of the commitments they made to God when they became a priest or nun. Buddhist monks are commonly seen in robes of various colors, which have symbolic meaning to them.

Comparing the "robes of the Holy Priesthood" to the sacred vestments of other religious traditions, The Church of Jesus Christ of Latter-day Saints has pointed out:

> Not all such religious vestments are on public display. Some are seen only in places of worship. Temple robes of The Church of Jesus Christ of Latter-day Saints, known as the robes of the Holy Priesthood, are worn only inside Mormon temples and [are] reserved for the highest sacraments of the faith.
>
> White symbolizes purity. There is no insignia or rank. The highest Apostle and the newest member are indistinguishable when dressed in the same way. Men and women wear similar clothing. The simple vestments combine religious symbolism with echoes of antiquity reflected in ancient writings from the book of Exodus.[4]

This comparison of modern Latter-day Saint temple clothes to the sacred clothing mentioned in the book of Exodus and worn by the priests of the ancient temple may be helpful in preparing you for what you will see in the temple.

The Robe (Exodus 28:4; Leviticus 8:7)

There are numerous references in the scriptures to people wearing robes, particularly in relation to them serving in the temple. While there are differences in the appearance of the robes worn by ancient temple priests and those worn in Latter-day Saint temples today, the principle is similar. This article of clothing worn by those who serve in the house of the Lord is highly symbolic. One source states, "In priestly tradition, special outerwear depicted power."[5] Anciently, robes were standard symbols for "the power of heaven" or priesthood, and the wearer was viewed as the "earthly representative" of God.[6] One expert in biblical clothing wrote, "Some traditions," both in the Old and New Testaments, "portray the outer garment of special persons as conveying power."[7] Latter-day Saints go to the temple to, among other things, be "endowed with power from on high" (D&C 105:11) and to become, as Joseph Smith taught, "a kingdom of priests [as] in Enoch's day."[8] The temple priesthood robes symbolically represent this concept.

The Ephod (Exodus 28:4, 6–7; Leviticus 8:7)

To date, there continues to be some debate within the scholarly community as to what exactly the ephod of the Old Testament was. Most scholars maintain that it was some kind of a colorful apron worn by temple priests.[9] Anciently, aprons sometimes served as symbols for "priesthood"[10] and "work."[11] It is likely for this reason that the High Priest, who served in the Mosaic tabernacle, was required to wear an apron or ephod (Exodus 28). He was engaged in the "work" of the Lord, a work that required that he be in possession of "priesthood" power. Of the Mosaic priest's apron and its relationship to the aprons of Adam and Eve, one source informs us:

> Adam and Eve, while in the garden, possessed two items of clothing that apparently held ritual meaning: the apron (Genesis 3:7) and the garment of skins (see Genesis 3:21). . . . No doubt [the apron] held some sort of ceremonial significance for the first couple. . . . It is quite likely that these vestments, belonging to Adam and Eve and obtained while in the garden, served as archetypes for later sacral vestments belonging to the Israelite temple system.[12]

Knowing that anciently aprons often symbolized "work," when you and I enter the house of the Lord, we go there to do very important and extremely sacred work: first for ourselves (and for our own salvation), and then we engage in work on behalf of our family and friends who have passed on before us.

The Girdle or Priestly Sash (Exodus 28:5–8; Leviticus 8:7)

In ancient times, both the Aaronic priests and the High Priest wore a "girdle" or "sash" around their waist as part of their priestly garments. In certain periods, in the ancient Near East, a girdle represented chastity and fidelity, including fidelity to covenants.[13]

Latter-day Saints should only enter into the higher covenants of the temple if they are committed to being faithful to those covenants, as the priestly sash suggests they will be.

The Miter and the Holy Crown
(Exodus 28:4, 39–40; 39:30–31; Leviticus 8:9)

The high priest of the ancient temple wore a cap or miter that was made of linen fabric. It was "of the distinctive design worn by royalty," meaning it carried the symbolism of the crown of a king.[14] Upon the front of the priest's miter was fastened the "Holy Crown," which consisted of a golden plate that bore the inscription "HOLINESS TO THE LORD" (Exodus 28:36). While there is no "holy crown" or "golden plate" attached to the caps men wear in temples today, the same symbolism is implied. These fabric caps are symbols of crowns, and remind us of the need for personal holiness if we are to become like the "King of Kings" (Revelation 17:14), and if we are to serve in His stead.

Veils (1 Corinthians 11:10)

While the ancient temple priests didn't wear veils, ancient "priestesses"—as they have been called—often did. The Apostle Paul explained that a woman "ought . . . to have power on her head because of the angels" (1 Corinthians 11:10). The Revised Standard Version of the Bible translates this verse: "The woman should have a veil on her head."[15] The Greek would be more accurately rendered "the woman should have *authority* on her head."[16] One source explains, "Far from being a symbol of the woman's subjection . . . her head-covering [or veil] is what Paul calls it—authority: in prayer and prophecy she, like the man, is [acting] under the authority of God."[17] One ancient source informs us, "The veil signifies power."[18] A woman wearing a veil, in certain contexts, can represent an authority or power that is divinely recognized.

As we clothe ourselves in these sacred and symbolic articles of clothing (common in the ancient Church as well as in the modern), we take upon ourselves both the role of priest/priestess and representative of Christ—and we make covenants that we will live out those roles by seeking to live lives of personal holiness.[19]

Notes

1. See "Sacred Temple Clothing," found at the official website of The Church of Jesus Christ of Latter-day Saints (https://www.lds.org/media-library/video/2014-01-1460-sacred-temple-clothing?lang=eng#d). © 2015 by Intellectual Reserve, Inc.

2. Adam S. Miller, *Letters to a Young Mormon*, second edition (Salt Lake City, UT: Deseret Book and the Maxwell Institute, 2007), 86.

3. Footnote 4d (in Exodus 28:4 of the 2013 LDS Scriptures) interprets the Hebrew word used in the passage (for "mitre") as a "cap."

4. "Sacred Temple Clothing," found at the official website of The Church of Jesus Christ of Latter-day Saints (https://www.lds.org/media-library/video/2014-01-1460-sacred-temple-clothing?lang=eng#d). © 2015 by Intellectual Reserve, Inc. You may want to use this video as a means of explaining to others why members of the Church wear special clothing in the temple.

5. Douglas R. Edwards, "Dress and Ornamentation," in David Noel Freedman, ed., *The Anchor Bible Dictionary* (New York: Doubleday, 1992), 2:233.

6. J. C. Cooper, *An Illustrated Encyclopaedia of Traditional Symbols* (London: Thames and Hudson, 1995), 140.

7. Douglas R. Edwards, "Dress and Ornamentation," in David Noel Freedman, ed., *The Anchor Bible Dictionary* (New York: Doubleday, 1992), 2:233 & 236.

8. Joseph Smith, "Nauvoo Relief Society Minute Book," March 31, 1842, in Jill Mulvay Derr, Carol Cornwall Madsen, Kate Holbrook, and Matthew Grown, *The First Fifty Years of Relief Society* (Salt Lake City, UT: The Church Historian's Press, 2016), 43.

9. See, for example, Carol Meyers, "Ephod," in *The Anchor Bible Dictionary*, David Noel Freedman, ed. (New York: Doubleday, 1992), 2:550; John L. McKenzie, *Dictionary of the Bible* (Milwaukee: The Bruce Publishing Company, 1965), 241; Allen C. Myers, ed., *The Eerdmans Bible Dictionary* (Grand Rapids, MI: Eerdmans, 1987), 342; Kaiser, "Exodus," 2:468; George Arthur Buttrick, ed., *The Interpreter's Bible* (New York: Abingdon Press, 1951–57), 1:1039; Michael D. Coogan, ed., *The New Oxford Annotated Bible*, 3rd ed. (New York: Oxford University Press, 2001), 122 (Hebrew Bible section). Some English translations render the Hebrew word "ephod" as "apron." See, for example, James Moffatt, trans., *A New Translation of The Bible: Containing the Old and New Testaments* (New York: Harper & Brothers, 1950), 92 (Hebrew Bible section); J. M. Powis Smith and Edgar J. Goodspeed, trans., *The Complete Bible: An American Translation* (Chicago: University of Chicago Press, 1949), 76 (Hebrew Bible section).

10. Keven J. Conner, *Interpreting the Symbols and Types* (Portland, OR: City Bible Publishing, 1992), 141; Merrill F. Unger, *Unger's Bible Dictionary* (Chicago, IL: Moody Press, 1966), 317.

11. Nadia Julien, *The Mammoth Dictionary of Symbols* (New York: Carroll and Graf Publishers, Inc., 1996), 23–24. J. C. Cooper, *An Illustrated Encyclopaedia of Traditional Symbols* (London: Thames and Hudson, 1995), 14.

12. Donald W. Parry, "Garden of Eden: Prototype Sanctuary," in Donald W. Parry, ed., *Temples of the Ancient World* (Provo, UT: Foundation for Ancient Research and Mormon Studies, 1994), 145.

13. See Douglas R. Edwards, "Dress and Ornamentation," in *The Anchor Bible Dictionary*, ed. David Noel Freedman (New York: Doubleday, 1992), 2:237; James Hall, *Dictionary of Subjects and Symbols in Art* (New York: Harper and Row, 1974), 138; Jack Tresidder, *Symbols and Their Meanings* (London: Duncan Baird Publishers, 2000), 134. See also J.C. Cooper, *An Illustrated Encyclopaedia of Traditional Symbols* (London: Thames and Hudson, 1995), 73–74; Hugh T. Henry, *Catholic Customs and Symbols* (New York: Benziger Brothers, 1925), 69–70.

14. See F. Brown, S. Driver, and C. Briggs, *The Brown-Driver-Briggs Hebrew and English Lexicon* (Peabody, MA: Hendrickson Publishers, 1999), 857, #4701. See also Matthew B. Brown, *The Gate of Heaven* (American Fork, UT: Covenants Communications, 1999), 84.

15. See also the *Joseph Smith Translation* of 1 Corinthians 11:10.

16. The *NIV, NRSV, The Jerusalem Bible*, and *New World Translation* also render the Greek word translated "power" in the *KJV* and "veil" in the *RSV* as "authority."

17. Leon Morris, *Tyndale New Testament Commentaries: 1 Corinthians*, revised edition (Grand Rapids, MI: Eerdmans, 1998), 152.

18. See Gerald Bray, ed., *Ancient Christian Commentary on Scripture: New Testament Volume 8, 1–2 Corinthians* (Downers Grove, IL: Inter-Varsity Press, 1999), 108.

19. For information on how each of the articles of clothing invite us to live more holy lives, see my article, "Clothed in Holy Garments: A Study of the Apparel of the Temple Officiants of Ancient Israel," in Alonzo L. Gaskill, *Temple Reflections: Insights Into The House of the Lord* (Springville, UT: Cedar Fort, 2016), 114–135.

{ 44 }

Where do I purchase the clothing I need to wear when I participate in my endowment? Or can I simply borrow or rent it?

In many parts of the world, the Church has *Distribution Services Stores* (often referred to as "distribution centers") that sell temple garments and other clothing worn in the temple. Your bishop, Relief Society president, or an endowed member of your ward or family will know if there is one near where you live.

If you happen to live in a part of the world where there is no Church distribution center, it is possible to order temple garments and other temple clothing online at www.store.lds.org.

If you have to order your temple clothing through the internet, make certain that you order what you need well in advance of the day that you will be receiving your endowment, just to ensure that they arrive in time for your special day.

In addition, if you have to order your garments and temple clothing online, it will be helpful to have sitting alongside of you as you place your order a person who has already received his or her own endowment. That way, you will be sure to get everything you need. (If you purchase your temple clothing at a Church distribution center, the employees there can help to ensure that you have everything you need.)

While it wouldn't be appropriate to borrow someone else's temple garments (i.e., underwear), it certainly would be acceptable to borrow someone else's other items of temple clothing. However, if you live close enough to a temple that you plan to attend regularly the rest of your life, and if you are financially able, there is wisdom in purchasing your own temple clothes. That will make it more convenient for you to attend whenever you would like, and it will ensure that you have clothing that is clean and fits you properly.

45

What covenants will I make when I receive my endowment?

When they receive their endowment, some people are surprised that the covenants they make in the temple are *not* about "new" or "secretive" things. For many, the covenants made in the temple feel like an expansion of what they already promised God at their baptism. President Harold B. Lee (1899–1973), eleventh President of the Church, explained, "The receiving of the endowment requires the assuming of obligations by covenants which in reality are but an embodiment or an unfolding of the covenants each person should have assumed at baptism."[1] Similarly, an article in the Church's *New Era* magazine explained, "The promises you as a member are asked to make [in the temple] will not surprise you. They are consistent with teachings you have already received, including obedience, sacrifice, order, love, chastity, and consecration."[2]

As you'll recall, when you were baptized, you made a covenant with God regarding how you would—from that day forward—seek to live a life of faithfulness. Implied in your baptismal covenant was a commitment that you would try to be *obedient* (Moses 5:1–6) to God's commandments. Additionally, in essence, you promised your Father in Heaven that you would seek to make whatever *sacrifices* (Moses 5:4–8, 20) He might call upon you to make. In being baptized, you were committing to try each day to live Christ's *higher law* (sometimes referred to as the "law of the Gospel" [Moses 5:58–59; 8:19]). Also included in the promises you made at baptism was a commitment that you would faithfully live the law of *chastity* (Moses 6:5–23; 8:13), and do all that you could to live a fully *consecrated life* (Moses 7:18). In a very real sense, during your baptism, you made a general covenant about who you would seek to become and how you would try to live your life. During your endowment, however, you will make more specific covenants—promises to your Heavenly Father that were inherent in your baptismal covenant, but not specifically articulated in detail at the time you were baptized.

President Ezra Taft Benson (1899–1994), thirteenth President of the Church, summarized the specific covenants each makes during the endowment in this way:

> Celestial laws, embodied in certain ordinances belonging to the Church of Jesus Christ, are complied with by voluntary covenants. The laws are spiritual. Thus, our father in Heaven has ordained certain holy sanctuaries, called temples, in which these laws may be fully explained, the laws include the law of obedience and sacrifice, the law of the gospel, the law of chastity, and the law of consecration.[3]

Similarly, speaking to the young men of the Aaronic Priesthood, Elder Robert D. Hales (1932–2017), of the Quorum of the Twelve Apostles, taught, "We are preparing ourselves to take on higher laws and covenants [of the temple] such as obedience, sacrifice, service, chastity, and consecration of our time and talents. Why do we do this? We should learn this before we go to the temple, brethren, because afterwards it will help each of us to be valiant missionaries, caring eternal companions, and devoted fathers."[4] In essence, President Benson, Elder Hales, and other General Authorities of the Church have laid out for each of us what we will commit to when we enter the holy temple and receive our sacred endowment.[5]

Using President Benson's list of temple covenants, let's *briefly* discuss what each of these entails. However, remember that it will be your responsibility—once you have received your endowment—to more fully examine each of these covenants, and to study them, so that you can learn how they pertain to your own life and what God expects of you.

♦ *The Law of Obedience:* In this covenant, you promise God that you will keep His commandments to the best of your ability. You will strive to be faithful to the Father in all things. The Prophet Joseph is purported to have said, "I made this my rule: When the Lord commands, do it."[6] Obedience doesn't imply perfection, but it does imply loyalty and striving to do God's will; it implies we are *willing*—as the sacrament prayer says— to keep the Lord's commandments. When seeking to keep this covenant, it may be helpful to keep in mind D&C 1:38, which states: "Whether by mine own voice or by the voice of my servants, it is the same." In other words, our commitment to be obedient should apply not only to the commandments of ancient times but also to the inspired words and counsel of modern representatives of the Lord Jesus Christ—our contemporary prophetic leaders.

♦ *The Law of Sacrifice:* Through this covenant we promise to follow the example of Jesus Christ, whose life was one of constant sacrifice. Christ *always* put the Father's will before His own, and through this covenant we are invited to do the same. In the *Lectures on Faith* we find the following principle— often attributed to the Prophet Joseph (1805–1844): "A religion that does not require the sacrifice of all things never has power sufficient to produce the faith necessary unto life and salvation; for . . . it was through this sacrifice, and this only, that God has ordained that men should enjoy eternal life."[7] Personal sacrifice is what makes us truly like God. Mother Teresa encapsulated the spirit of this covenant when she said, "Take whatever [God] gives and give whatever He takes with a big smile . . ." Be willing "to be used by Him as it pleases *Him*."[8] If we fully live the law of sacrifice, we are willing to let God "take" whatever He needs from us and to "give" or "do" whatever He asks of us—even if it requires great sacrifice on our part.

♦ *The Law of the Gospel:* This law is sometimes placed in juxtaposition with the law of Moses—or lesser law. Thus, President David O. McKay (1873–1970), ninth President of the Church, referred to "the Law of the Gospel," saying it was "the power of God unto salvation."[9] One Latter-day Saint scholar explained this law as follows:

Although the law of the Gospel is never expressly defined in scripture, I understand this law to be the law of love and generosity: "Thou shalt love the Lord thy God with all thy heart, and with all thy soul, and with all thy mind. This is the first and great commandment, and the second is like unto it, Thou shalt love thy neighbor as thyself" (Matthew 22:37–39; quoting Deuteronomy 6:5; see also D&C 59:506). "Therefore, if any man shall take of the abundance which I have made, and impart not his portion, according to *the law of my gospel,* unto the poor and the needy, he shall, with the wicked, lift up his eyes in hell, being in torment" (D&C 104:18; italics added).[10]

Thus, this covenant is typically understood to mean that you promise you will try to live the higher teachings of Jesus—including the command to learn to manifest God's love for His children in every aspect of our lives (see Matthew 5–7; 3 Nephi 11–12; Mosiah 4).

♦ *The Law of Chastity:* Through this covenant, you promise God that you will be sexually pure in your actions and thoughts. You covenant not to engage in any sexual relations outside of marriage and to live a life that is morally pure in *all aspects*—as defined by the Lord and His prophets. One fully lives the law of chastity when one is modest in dress; moral and appropriate in relationships; and circumspect in words, in thoughts, and even in what one views.

♦ *The Law of Consecration:* Through this covenant, we promise God that all aspects of our lives belong to Him and that we will use our lives to do His holy will.[11] Elder Bruce R. McConkie (1915–1985), a former member of the Quorum of the Twelve Apostles, said that this law means "that we consecrate our time, our talents, and our money and property to the cause of the Church; such are to be available to the extent they are needed to further the Lord's interests on earth."[12] This covenant goes beyond faithfully paying our tithing—though it includes that. It suggests that if you have talents or gifts, those belong to the Lord and should be used for His purposes. Even your time belongs to the Lord, and it should be used—where possible—to bless the lives of His children and to help build His kingdom. This covenant implies that as you contemplate education and employment, you will do so in the context of how the Lord might best use you—with your particular talents and gifts—to do His will, and then you will choose your educational path and employment accordingly. President McKay explained, "My time, my talents, and all that I possess, are placed upon the altar for the advancement of the kingdom of God."[13] Through this covenant, we let the Lord know that we are fully vested in His work and will, and that our own goals are secondary to His ultimate goal—the salvation of His children (see Moses 1:39).

Once you have received your endowment, if you will study each of these covenants—and what the scriptures and living prophets have taught about them—your Father in Heaven will make it clear to you how you can most fully live these promises you have made to the Lord.

In addition, remember that each covenant you enter into also has promised blessings attached to it—*if* you faithfully keep the promises you made to the Lord. Just as you are under obligation to study each of the covenants you have entered into, you should also seek out a fuller understanding of the remarkable promised blessings the Lord offers you through obedience to the laws that He has asked you to keep. As you study your covenants and their associated blessings, you will be overwhelmed with the Lord's mercy and generosity in using these covenants to protect you and richly bless you.

Notes

1. Harold B. Lee, *The Teachings of Harold B.* Lee (Salt Lake City, UT: Bookcraft, 1998), 574.
2. "Q&A: Questions and Answers," in *New Era* (January 1994), 18.
3. Ezra Taft Benson, "A Vision and a Hope for the Youth of Zion," in *Brigham Young University, Speeches of the Year*, April 12, 1977, BYU Devotional, 1. See Ezra Taft Benson, *Teachings of Ezra Taft Benson* (Salt Lake City, UT: Bookcraft, 1998), 121.
4. Robert D. Hales, "The Aaronic Priesthood: Return with Honor," in *Ensign*, May 1990, 39.
5. For a list of specific covenants made in the temple, which prophets and apostles have outlined for members of the Church, see the following publications: Ezra Taft

Benson, *The Teachings of Ezra Taft Benson* (Salt Lake City, UT: Bookcraft, 1998), 121; Bruce R. McConkie, *Doctrines of the Restoration: The Sermons and Writings of Bruce R. McConkie*, Mark L. McConkie, compiler (Salt Lake City, UT: Bookcraft, 1989), 384; Ezra Taft Benson, *The Teachings of Ezra Taft Benson* (Salt Lake City, UT: Bookcraft, 1998), 121; James E. Faust, "Who Shall Ascend into the Hill of the Lord?" in *Ensign*, August 2001, 4; Eldred G. Smith, Discourse delivered March 10, 1964 at Brigham Young University, in *BYU Speeches of the Year* (1964), 8; Gordon B. Hinckley, *Teachings of Gordon B. Hinckley* (Salt Lake City, UT: Deseret Book, 1997), 147; David O. McKay, "An Address on the Temple Ceremony," given to missionaries at the Salt Lake Temple Annex, Thursday, September 25, 1941, Harold B. Lee Library, Special Collections, Brigham Young University, 2–3; James E. Talmage, *The House of the Lord* (Salt Lake City, UT: The Church of Jesus Christ of Latter-day Saints, 2013), 88; Jeffrey R. Holland, "Keeping Covenants: A Message for Those Who Will Serve a Mission," in *New Era*, January 2012, 4; Robert D. Hales, "The Aaronic Priesthood: Return with Honor," in *Ensign*, May 1990, 39; Ezra Taft Benson, "A Vision and a Hope for the Youth of Zion," in *Brigham Young University, Speeches of the Year*, April 12, 1977, BYU Devotional, 1. See also Hugh Nibley, *Approaching Zion* (Provo/Salt Lake City, UT: Foundation for Ancient Research and Mormon Studies/Deseret Book, 1989), 441–2; Immo Luschin, "Latter-day Saint Temple Worship and Activity, in *Encyclopedia of Mormonism*, Daniel H. Ludlow, ed., four volumes (New York: Macmillan, 1994), 4:1447; Alma P. Burton, "Endowment," in Ludlow (1994), 2:455; Jeffrey M. Bradshaw, "The Five Celestial Laws," in Jeffery M. Bradshaw, *Temple Themes in the Book of Moses* (Salt Lake City, UT: Eborn Books, 2010), 203–216.

6.   Joseph Smith, in *History of the Church*, seven volumes, B. H. Roberts, ed. (Salt Lake City, UT: Deseret Book, 1978), 2:170.

7.   *Lectures on Faith* 6:7. See 6:5–12 and 7:20.

8.   Mother Teresa, *Where There Is Love, There Is God* (New York: Image, 2010), 299, emphasis added.

9.   See David O. McKay, "An Address on the Temple Ceremony," given to missionaries at the Salt Lake Temple Annex, Thursday, September 25, 1941. Harold B. Lee Library, Special Collections, Brigham Young University, 3.

10.   John W. Welch, *The Sermon at the Temple and the Sermon on the Mount* (Salt Lake City, UT: Deseret Book, 1990), 56–57.

11.   See Ezra Taft Benson, *Teachings of Ezra Taft Benson* (Salt Lake City, UT: Bookcraft, 1998), 121.

12.   Bruce R. McConkie, "Obedience, Consecration, and Sacrifice," in *Ensign*, May 1975, 50.

13.   David O. McKay, "An Address on the Temple Ceremony," given to missionaries at the Salt Lake Temple Annex, Thursday, September 25, 1941. Harold B. Lee Library, Special Collections, Brigham Young University, 3.

46

Will I learn lots of new doctrine when I receive my endowment?

Most people, when they receive their endowment, are surprised at how familiar much of what they are taught in the temple is. Of course, God's doctrine doesn't change—and in the Church, we do not have "secret doctrines." Consequently, the doctrine you will be taught in the temple should sound familiar and fit right in with what you have been taught much of your life.

The primary difference between what is taught in the temple and what you've learned at Church over the years has to do with how the teachings are packaged. From the pulpit at Church, and in our Sunday classrooms, the doctrine is presented in pretty straightforward ways. In the temple, the doctrine is sometimes presented in very symbolic ways. Until one looks past the outward forms, and really thinks about the symbols, one might think that the message is some new or mysterious doctrine. However, it is not; it is simply presented, much like Jesus's parables, so that the more spiritually prepared we are, the more we will receive from the things we are taught in the house of the Lord.[1]

Note

1. See Bruce R. McConkie, *Mormon Doctrine*, second edition (Salt Lake City, UT: Bookcraft, 1979), 553.

47

I've heard that the story of the Creation and the Fall are told each time you participate in an endowment session. Why is that?

The endowment has frequently been described as "a ritualized depiction of humankind's journey from the premortal existence through earth life and beyond."[1] Central to that universal journey is the Creation and the Fall of Adam and Eve, which symbolically mirror our divine creation and our individual falls from grace.[2]

In the story of the Creation, we learn about how God took the chaos that existed in space and organized it—bringing order to the universe and to our world. In the story of the Fall, we learn about how humans, through hearkening unto Satan, reintroduce chaos into the world and into their lives. Each time we attend the temple and see depicted for us the stories of the Creation and the Fall of Adam and Eve, we should put ourselves into Adam and Eve's shoes. We should think of these two stories as *our own* stories and ask ourselves how (through listening to the devil) we have created chaos in our own lives.

As the endowment progresses, we sense that Christ is the answer to the chaos in our lives; He is the answer to each of the wrong choices we make. The temple endowment explains for us how we can overcome the chaos and bring order and peace back into our lives, through hearkening unto Christ and His commandments—and through entering into and keeping sacred covenants.

Notes

1. See, for example, Gregory A. Prince and William Robert Wright, *David O. McKay and the Rise of Modern Mormonism* (Salt Lake City, UT: University of Utah Press, 2001), 277.

2. Ed J. Pinegar, *The Temple: Gaining Knowledge and Power in the House of the Lord* (American Fork, UT: Covenant Communications, 2014), 12–24.

48

How long will it take to receive my endowment?

A typical endowment session takes less than two hours, in addition to whatever time you spend in the celestial room of the temple after you have completed the endowment ceremony. However, on the day you receive your endowment, you and your escort will need to arrive at the temple about seventy-five to ninety minutes before your endowment session starts in order to participate in a few preliminary things. (When you call to schedule your endowment, the temple worker will let you know exactly how early you need to arrive.) Thus, you should plan to be in the temple for approximately *three and a half to four hours* on the day you receive your own endowment.

President Boyd K. Packer (1924–2015)—former President of the Quorum of the Twelve Apostles—suggested you should do all that you can to not be late to the temple on the day that you receive your endowment. He noted that getting to the temple "early is not just for . . . making sure that the recommends and other things are in order and that we can adapt ourselves to the new experience. It is more than that. It is to get into the right place in time to get *calmly* into the right spirit—to get ourselves prepared for what is to take place."[1] Similarly, Elder Craig C. Christensen, of the Seventy, recently counseled that after you finish an endowment session in the temple, you should spend some time in the celestial room worshiping your Father in Heaven—rather than rushing out of the temple as soon as your endowment session is completed.[2] It will be difficult to have a spirit of calm and peace about you if you are rushing because you arrived late to the temple or if you are in a hurry to get out of the temple after completing your endowment session.

When you first arrive, there will typically be a temple worker waiting for you near the front desk (where patrons present their temple recommends). That sister or brother will have a list of all those who will be receiving their own endowment that day. Since you will have called and made an appointment to receive your endowment, your name will be on that list.

Next, a staff member will review your temple recommend and records to make sure there are no mistakes on them. After those initial bits of paperwork are taken care of, you and your escort will go to the locker room to change out of your street clothes and put on the white clothing each patron (or participant) wears in the temple.

At that point you will receive your initiatory ordinances (that we spoke about in Question #25), after which you will have a meeting with a member of the temple presidency (if you are a male) or (if you are a female) one of the temple matrons (who are the wives of the members of the temple presidency). They will teach you a bit about the temple.

Finally, once all of that is completed, you and your escort will make your way to the room in which you will begin the remainder of the endowment. (There you will meet up with the guests you invited to be with you in the temple that day.) In that ordinance room, you will spend the next one and a half to two hours making covenants and receiving instructions. (In some temples you will get up and go into a different room at various stages of the endowment. However, in other temples the bulk of the endowment is performed in a singular ordinance room.) At the conclusion of the endowment ceremony, you will have time in the celestial room to quietly converse with the family or friends that were with you when you received your endowment. It is there, in the room that represents God's highest heaven, that you can reverently discuss temple-related matters with other endowed members of the

Church and where you can spend time in quiet contemplation, prayer, and worship.

Because you will be in the temple for an extended period of time on your first time through an endowment ceremony, there is wisdom in eating before you arrive. There is also value in using the restroom just after you receive your initiatory ordinances but before you begin the lengthiest portion of your endowment. You would not want your hunger or your need to use the restroom to distract you from your sacred experience in the temple.

Notes

1. Boyd K. Packer, *The Holy Temple* (Salt Lake City, UT: Bookcraft, 1980), 65, emphasis added.
2. Craig C. Christensen, in Leadership Conference—First Session, December 1, 2018, Payson, UT.

49

Should I receive both my endowment and sealing on the same day?

You are certainly allowed to receive your endowment and sealing on the same day, if you so choose—and some do. However, since receiving your own endowment can take as many as four hours (when you combine the interviews, initiatory, and endowment ceremony), being sealed on that same day would add another hour to the length of time you will be in the temple. On top of that, many wish to take pictures outside of the temple (with family and friends) on the day they are sealed. That could easily require that you be at the temple for six hours straight (if you choose to receive your endowment and sealing ordinances on the same day). Consequently, you may want to discuss this with the person you will be sealed to and determine if this is the right thing for each of you. If you are already married and you have little children who will be sealed to you, this will also take some additional planning.

If you decide to receive your endowment and sealing on different days, on the day of your sealing, you (and your escorts and witnesses) will need to arrive at the temple about seventy-five to ninety minutes before the time of your scheduled sealing. When you call to schedule your sealing, the temple will inform you of how early you need to arrive. (Guests who will be attending your sealing are encouraged to be in the marriage waiting room of the temple a minimum of thirty minutes before the scheduled sealing.) Because you will have scheduled the sealing ceremony with the temple in advance of the day you are being sealed, there will be a temple worker in the foyer near where you present your temple recommend who will be expecting you—and who will have a list of all sealings being performed in the temple that day. That worker will find you on the list, and then a member of the temple staff will take you into an interview room and review all of your paperwork to ensure that everything is in order prior to your actual sealing. After that short meeting, you will each be escorted to separate dressing rooms, where you will change into your temple clothing, after which you will be escorted to the sealing room, where your guests will be waiting for you and where you will be sealed for time and for all eternity. (Contingent upon when the two of you received your own endowments, it is possible that you may also participate in a short rite *before* entering the sealing room [see Question #58]. This is a simple, brief, and private ceremony between the bride and groom that is performed for those who received their endowment quite some time prior to the day of their sealing.)

Sealing ceremonies typically take between twenty-five and forty-five minutes, in addition to the interview time and the time required for the two of you to change into your temple clothing.

50

Why is there so much secrecy surrounding what goes on in the temple?

Members of the Church commonly say that the ordinances of the temple are "sacred, not secret." While that is certainly true, there is definitely a culture in the Church of not talking much about what goes on in the temple when outside of the temple. There are probably several reasons why that is.

If we are completely honest, one of the biggest reasons people are so secretive about what happens in the temple is because they say they are not sure what they can or cannot say—so they just don't say *anything*. As we will discuss in Question #52, you are told in the temple exactly what you can or cannot speak of outside of the walls of the temple. However, some members neglect to pay attention to that instruction and, therefore, find themselves unsure.

Another reason we are so careful about what we speak of outside of the temple is explained by this statement from the Prophet Joseph (1805–1844): "The reason we do not have the secrets of the Lord revealed unto us, is because we do not keep them but reveal them; we do not keep our own secrets, but reveal [them] to the world, even to our enemies, then how would we keep the secrets of the Lord? I can keep a secret till Doomsday."[1] The Prophet was suggesting that sacred things should be kept sacred so that the Lord can trust us. Once we have proven to God that we can keep to ourselves the sacred things He reveals to us in the temple, then He will reveal more to us. If we wish the temple to be for us "a house of learning [and] a house of glory"—even a place of personal revelation—then we need to reverence the sacred things we learn therein.

Not talking openly about the details of what goes on in the temple can actually enhance our reverence for them. If you limit your detailed discussion about sacred things to specific sacred spaces, then those things continue to feel holy to you. However, if you casually talk about them in just any setting, they may begin to feel less sacred and less special.

Related to the previous idea is the fact that treating temple matters as sacred helps to keep them from being driven into popular culture. As Latter-day Saint scholar Hugh Nibley (1910–2005) pointed out:

> The scriptural injunction to secrecy (see Psalm 25:14; Amos 3:7; Proverbs 3:32) follows from the stringent necessity of keeping a discrete distance from the world. "Pearls before swine" is not an expression of contempt, but a commentary on the uselessness of giving things to people who place no value on them, have no use for them, and could only spoil them. . . . But for [us Latter-day Saints], there is no appeal whatever in secrecy as such. Sacred things, if freely discussed in public, would invariably be distorted, vulgarized, misinterpreted beyond recognition, and so lost.[2]

As an example of what Hugh Nibley was speaking of, the cross—which is a symbol of Jesus's ultimate sacrifice—has become popular as jewelry, not simply among believing Christians, but also among celebrities who do not hold it sacred. Thus, what was originally intended as a symbol of the most sacred event in the history of the world has now become a cheap and gaudy symbol of a culture that has nothing to do with God and everything to do with worldliness. Consequently, as you and I protect what goes on in the temple—and reverence it with all of our hearts—this will increase the likelihood that it will not be mistreated in the way that other religious symbols, like the cross, have been.

Notes

1. Joseph Smith, *Teachings of the Prophet Joseph Smith*, Joseph Fielding Smith, compiler (Salt Lake City, UT: Deseret Book, 1976), 195.
2. Hugh Nibley, "On the Sacred and the Symbolic," in Donald W. Parry, *Temples of the Ancient World* (Provo/Salt Lake City, UT: Foundation for Ancient Research and Mormon Studies/Deseret Book, 1994), 553–54.

51

I hear members of the Church who have received their endowment talk about "tokens" and "signs." What is that all about?

In the Church, we tend to use words that are unique to Latter-day Saints—words which don't necessarily mean much to those outside of our faith. For example, a non-Mormon isn't likely to know what a member of The Church of Jesus Christ of Latter-day Saints is talking about if she refers to "the stake center," "name extraction," or "area seventies." Some of these terms are uniquely LDS, and they simply do not mean much to those who are not of our faith.

Similarly, in the temple we have terms we use that do not mean much to those who have not yet received their endowment. The words "sign" and "token" are good examples of this.[1] One author explained, "The word *symbol* is of ancient Greek derivation and means, literally, a 'token' or 'sign' or 'something compared to something else.'"[2] As explained earlier in this book (see Questions #6 & 7), in the temple we use many symbols as a means of conveying doctrinal ideas. Signs and tokens are just religious symbols that are part of the temple endowment.[3] They are designed to help us to think more deeply about what the endowment symbolizes or means, and to help us to know that God promises to *always* keep His covenants with us. President David O. McKay (1873–1970), ninth President of the Church, explained, "There are certain things which belong to the Priesthood, signs and tokens that belong to the priesthood, which will emphasize the importance of the covenants you make" in the temple.[4] Similarly, the Prophet Joseph (1805–1844) explained that there are "certain key words & signs belonging to the priesthood which must be observed in order to obtain the blessings" offered in the holy endowment.[5]

In modern times, one sees symbolic signs in ordinances, such as baptism, where the person performing the ordinance makes a sign by raising his right arm to the square. In ancient times, the most sacred symbols were often referred to as signs or tokens—and they were commonly used as part of making covenants.[6] For example, in Genesis chapter 9, God gave Noah a "*token* of the covenant" that He was entering into with the prophet (Genesis 9:12, 17, emphasis added).[7] Heavenly Father did something similar with Abraham, stating that the symbol or sign given to Abraham by God would function as "a *token* of the covenant" between the two of them (Genesis 17:11). The Hebrew word translated as *token* in both of these passages means literally a "sign," "symbol," or "proof."[8] By giving Noah and Abraham a token, God was saying, in effect, "By this symbol (*token*), Noah/Abraham, I am *proving* to you that I will keep my covenant with you."

Making symbolic gestures or signs during the covenant-making process was common in most ancient societies. One Latter-day Saint source explained:

> Religious rituals (or rites) are sacred actions or "ceremonial movements." Some scholars refer to these rites of transition as "gestures of approach" because they are religious gestures (or acts or movements) that worshipers make as they approach God during sacred worship. The ancient temple, especially, included sacred gestures that enabled and empowered worshipers to move from the outer gate inward to the most holy place of all, the holy of holies. The gestures of approach are vital to a temple society because they symbolically cleanse and prepare worshipers for entry into and movement through sacred space as they transition from the profane world into the sacred temple.[9]

In other words, in ancient temples, the participants in the ordinances made certain signs, gestures, and symbolic movements as a means of representing that they were preparing themselves to enter into the presence of God. This explains what President Boyd K. Packer (1924–2015), former President of the Quorum of the Twelve Apostles, meant when he taught that at the end of our lives, "we shall approach the veil and there, with *signs* and *tokens* given, we will be extended the sublimest of all invitations: 'Enter into the joy of thy Lord.'"[10] It is also what President Brigham Young (1801–1877), second President of the Church, meant when he said, "Your endowment is, to receive all those ordinances in the house of the Lord, which are necessary for you, after you have departed this life, to enable you to walk back to the presence of the Father, passing the angels who stand as sentinels, being enabled to give them the key words, the *signs* and *tokens*, pertaining to the holy Priesthood, and gain your eternal exaltation."[11]

In ancient times, one of the most common forms of these symbols or "gestures of approach" was a sacred handclasp. Latter-day Saint author, Stephen D. Ricks, spoke of "a solemn and ceremonial handclasp" known by the Greeks as *dexiosis*, and in Latin as *dextrarum iunctio*, which means "giving" or "joining of [the] right hands." Dr. Ricks noted the commonality of these "gestures" or "tokens" in ancient times when taking an oath of allegiance, or when receiving sacred ordinances sometimes called "the mysteries." Indeed, he points out that initiates into these ordinances were typically called *syndexioi*, meaning those who were "joined by the right hand."[12] This explains why, in the Joseph Smith Translation of Genesis 24:2 & 8, we read, "And Abraham said unto his eldest servant of his house . . . Put forth I pray thee thy hand under my hand, and I will make thee swear before the Lord, the God of heaven, and the God of the earth . . . And the servant put his hand under the hand of Abraham his master, and sware to him concerning that matter." Abraham was here making a covenant with his servant and did so by clasping hands with his servant as they swore an oath together. The giving of the hand showed that a relationship had been established between two persons. (See 2 Kings 10:15; Jeremiah 50:15; Ezekiel 17:18.) Anciently, to clasp another's hand was a symbol of a "pledge" or an expression of "solidarity." And so it is today. In modern Western culture the handshake represents a pledge or promise. We commonly shake hands as a means of offering an assurance that we will keep a commitment we have made. This modern practice likely stems from the ancient religious rite described above.

In discussing how this principle applies to members of The Church of Jesus Christ of Latter-day Saints, Elder Matthew Cowley (1897–1953), of the Quorum of the Twelve Apostles, explained:

> There flashed in my mind . . . the symbol which is over the long narrow window on the east and west end of that great [Salt Lake] temple, the symbol of the clasped hands. How important that symbol is in the lives of all of us! We men of the priesthood who have knelt at the sacred altar and on that altar clasped the hand of a sainted companion . . . have entered an eternal triangle, not a companionship of two but of three[—]the husband, the wife and God—the most sacred triangle man and woman can become a part of. . . . We pledge eternal fidelity to one another as we kneel at the sacred altar, and the words we hear are not "until death do you part," nor "for as long as you both shall life," but "for time and for all eternity."[13]

Handclasp above window of the center tower of the east and west faces of the Salt Lake Temple

The act of giving one's hand when making a covenant was taken quite seriously in ancient times. It suggested that you were giving your solemn promise (represented by your hand) that you would *not* break your covenant *for anything*—not even to spare your own life.[14] Thus, in Ezekiel 17:18 we read, "Seeing he despised the oath by breaking the covenant, when, lo, *he had given his hand,* and hath done all these things, he shall not escape." This verse informs us of a man who apparently despised God and his covenants, for he had "given his hand" in *token* of the covenant he had made, and yet he broke his promise. Consequently, Ezekiel informs us, "he shall not escape" punishment for breaking his covenant.

Anciently, *signs* and *tokens* helped to convey sacred truths, create a relationship of unity between parties, bind the initiate in a covenant relationship with God, and hold him or her accountable for the promises made via the clasping of hands.

Notes

1. See Todd Compton, "Symbolism," in *Encyclopedia of Mormonism,* Daniel H. Ludlow, ed., four volumes (New York: Macmillan, 1994), 3:1430; Andrew C. Skinner, *Temple Worship: 20 Truths That Will Bless Your Life* (Salt Lake City, UT: Deseret Book, 2001), 112–113.

2. Andrew C. Skinner, *Temple Worship: 20 Truths That Will Bless Your Life* (Salt Lake City, UT: Deseret Book, 2001), 175.

3. Brigham Young stated, "We want to build the Temple so as to get our endowment, and if we do our best, and Satan will not let us build it, we will go into the wilderness and we will receive the Endowment, for we will receive an endowment anyhow . . . We have all the signs and tokens to give to the porter at the door, and he will let us in" heaven. Discourse given August 8, 1844, Nauvoo, IL, in *The Complete Discourses of Brigham Young,* five volumes, Richard S. Van Wagoner, ed. (Salt Lake City, UT: The Smith-Pettit Foundation, 1999), 1:43, emphasis added. See also Boyd K. Packer, *Our Father's Plan,* rev. ed. (Salt Lake City: Deseret Book, 1994), 46; Joseph F. Smith, December 16, 1905 letter to Alvin, Chase, George and Willard Smith, in *From Prophet to Son: Advice of Joseph F. Smith to His Missionary Sons,* Hyrum M. Smith III and Scott G. Kenney, compilers (Salt Lake City, UT: Deseret Book, 1981), 93; Joseph Smith, discourse given March 20, 1842, in *The Words of Joseph Smith—The Contemporary Accounts of the Nauvoo Discourse of the Prophet Joseph,* Andrew F. Ehat and Lyndon W. Cook, compilers (Provo, UT: Religious Studies Center, Brigham Young University, 1980), 108; Brigham Young, discourse given May 24, 1863, in *Journal of Discourses,* 10:172; Brigham Young, discourse given April 6, 1853, in *Journal of Discourses* 2:31; Brigham Young, discourse given February 14, 1853, in *Journal of Discourses* 1:278; Hugh Nibley, *Teachings of the Book of Mormon,* 4 vols. (Provo, Utah: Foundation for Ancient Research and Mormon Studies, 2004), 1:204. (See also 1:242.); William Clayton, journal entry for December 13, 1845, in *An Intimate Chronicle: The Journals of William Clayton,* George D. Smith, compilers (Salt Lake City, UT: Signature Books, 1991), 210.

4. David O. McKay, "An Address on the Temple Ceremony," given to missionaries at the Salt Lake Temple Annex, Thursday, September 25, 1941. Harold B. Lee Library, Special Collections, Brigham Young University, 3. President McKay addressed

these remarks to missionaries *prior* to their receiving their endowment—and *not* actually in the temple itself, but in the annex next to the temple.

5. Joseph Smith, discourse given March 20, 1842, in *The Words of Joseph Smith—The Contemporary Accounts of the Nauvoo Discourse of the Prophet Joseph*, Andrew F. Ehat and Lyndon W. Cook, compilers (Provo, UT: Religious Studies Center, Brigham Young University, 1980), 108.

6. See Andrew C. Skinner, *Temple Worship: 20 Truths That Will Bless Your Life* (Salt Lake City, UT: Deseret Book, 2001), 112–113.

7. See Richard H. Morley, *A Scriptural Glossary of Manti Temple Terms* (Price, UT: Wix Plaza Book Sales, 2004), 75.

8. See Francis Brown, S. R. Driver and Charles A. Briggs, *The Brown-Driver-Briggs Hebrew and English Lexicon* (Peabody, MA: Hendrickson Publishers, 1999), 16.

9. Donald W. Parry and Jay A. Parry, *Symbols & Shadows: Unlocking a Deeper Understanding of the Atonement* (Salt Lake City, UT: Deseret Book, 2009), 22.

10. Boyd K. Packer, *Our Father's Plan*, rev. ed. (Salt Lake City: Deseret Book, 1994), 46, emphasis added.

11. Brigham Young made this comment at a public event in which the Church celebrated the beginning of the construction of the Salt Lake Temple. See Brigham Young, *Discourses of Brigham Young*, John A. Widtsoe, compiler (Salt Lake City, UT: Bookcraft, 1998), 416, emphasis added. Ed J. Pinegar pointed out, "Brigham Young's definition [of the endowment] applies to all the ordinances of the temple, including the initiatory ordinances, the endowment ceremony, and the sealing ordinances." Ed J. Pinegar, *The Temple: Gaining Knowledge and Power in the House of the Lord* (American Fork, UT: Covenant Communications, 2014), 104.

12. See Stephen D. Ricks, "*Dexiosis and Dextrarum Iunctio*: The Sacred Handclasp in the Classical and Early Christian World," in *The FARMS Review* 18/1 (2006): 431 & 432.

13. Matthew Cowley, in *Conference Report*, October 1952, 27.

14. In scripture oaths are traditionally made with the understanding that the one making the covenant sees his or her life on the line, should he or she break the covenant made. See for example, Ruth 1:16–17; 1 Nephi 4:32; Moses 5:29; JST Genesis 5:14. See also Edward F. Campbell, Jr., *The Anchor Bible: Ruth* (New York: Doubleday, 1975), 74; Hugh Nibley, *Temple And Cosmos: Beyond This Ignorant Present* (Provo, UT: Foundation for Ancient Research and Mormon Studies, 1992), 57–58.

52

Once I've received my endowment, what can I talk about outside of the temple?

We should be reverent about *everything* that goes on in the temple—including the covenants we make, the clothing we wear, and the things we learn. What transpires in the house of the Lord is among the most sacred instruction upon the face of the earth.

That being said, many members of the Church struggle to know what they can or cannot talk about once outside of the temple. Certainly one should try to avoid using specific temple language outside of the temple, if for no other reason than to prevent making what is said in the temple feel commonplace or ordinary and, thus, less sacred. However, in a spirit of reverence, there is much that *can* be discussed. Here are a few things to consider. Certainly, you *can* speak respectfully about the clothing worn therein, as the Church has released a video titled "Sacred Temple Clothing,"[1] which actually shows temple robes and temple garments, and a non–Latter-day Saint is welcome to attend the funeral of an endowed member of the Church and see him or her lying in the casket dressed in temple robes. Clearly, you *can* in reverential tones talk about the various covenants made in the temple, as a number of general authorities—including presidents of the Church—have done so in rather public venues.[2] Also, we know that the text of the video presentation or play that is depicted in the temple endowment comes almost word-for-word from the books of Genesis, Moses, and Abraham. Thus, it too *can* be read, reverently discussed, and contemplated outside of the temple. Therefore, while members of the Church adopt a range of attitudes on what can or cannot be discussed outside of the temple, it is worth noting that the list of things we have made a covenant to not discuss is actually quite limited.

In the endowment (which includes the initiatory ordinances), you make a covenant to not discuss in detail (outside of the temple) only a small handful of things. What you promise to not reveal pertains to things you "receive" in the temple, not to things you "learn." As noted previously, President Boyd K. Packer (1924–2015), former President of the Quorum of the Twelve Apostles, taught that, at the end of our lives, "We shall approach the veil and there, with *signs* and *tokens* given, we will be extended the sublimest of all invitations: 'Enter into the joy of thy Lord.'"[3] It is these *signs* and *tokens* that we do not reveal, nor do we discuss, outside of the holy temple. In addition, the "new name" (discussed in Question #32) is something we make a covenant to keep sacred once we have received it.

Latter-day Saint scholar, Hugh Nibley (1905–2005), expressed concern about the tendency for members of the Church to not discuss *anything* that goes on in the temple. He wrote: "The temple is definitely a school, a very *high* school of intense study, as temples in the past have been . . . Study is personal but your own thoughts, which may be helpful to others, *should* be exchanged as you 'teach one another' [D&C 109:7]—learning is a two-way process. Lest you be keeping something of value locked in your bosom, the temple gives you the opportunity to share what excites you."[4] Nibley certainly agreed that *some things* received in the temple should not be discussed outside of the temple. However, his bigger concern was that things we *can* talk about—and *should* talk about—often are *not* discussed and, thus, learning is stifled. D&C 63:64 informs us, "Remember that that which cometh from above is sacred, and must be spoken with care, and by constraint of the Spirit; *and in this* there is no condemnation . . ." This could certainly be applied to what we do in the temple. That which God has given *should* be held sacred, and *should* be spoken of with care. However, if we speak "with care" and under the "constraint" or influence "of the Spirit," then we can talk appropriately about those things that we have *not* made a covenant to keep secret.

Of course, the best place to talk about the temple is in the temple itself. However, I remind the reader of what was stated in the introduction to this book. President Ezra Taft Benson (1899–1994), thirteenth President of the Church, expressed his concern about how poorly we prepare the youth for their temple experience. He said:

> Because of its sacredness we are sometimes reluctant to say *anything* about the temple to our children and grandchildren. As a consequence, many do not develop a real desire to go to the temple, or when they go there, they do so without much background to prepare them for the obligations and covenants they enter into.
>
> I believe a proper understanding or background will immeasurably help prepare our youth for the temple.[5]

Similarly, President Packer wrote, "Lacking knowledge, some [who have not been through the temple] develop strange explanations about the work of our temples."[6] Also, the First Presidency of the Church expressed the following concern: "It has come to our attention that many of those planning to go to the temple for the first time are not properly oriented as to what to expect there. Under such circumstances they may fail to receive adequate understanding from their experience in the temple."[7] Thus, while we should be cautious and reverent about *everything* associated with the temple, parents, grandparents, and siblings need to do a better job of preparing their children, grandchildren, and siblings for what they will experience in the temple—so that they will have a positive and meaningful experience. In addition, once we have made the various covenants of the temple ourselves, we need to do a better job of helping each other understand the implications and meanings of what we experience in the temple. This will require that we talk more frequently about the temple—*not* about those things we have made a covenant to not reveal, but about the other components of the house of the Lord that we *are* allowed to discuss outside of the temple.

Notes

1. This video can be found in the media library at lds.org.

2. For a list of specific covenants made in the temple, which prophets and apostles have outlined for members of the Church, see the following publications: Ezra Taft Benson, *The Teachings of Ezra Taft Benson* (Salt Lake City, UT: Bookcraft, 1998), 121; Bruce R. McConkie, *Doctrines of the Restoration: The Sermons and Writings of Bruce R. McConkie*, Mark L. McConkie, compiler (Salt Lake City, UT: Bookcraft, 1989), 384; Ezra Taft Benson, *The Teachings of Ezra Taft Benson* (Salt Lake City, UT: Bookcraft, 1998), 121; James E. Faust, "Who Shall Ascend into the Hill of the Lord?" in *Ensign*, August 2001, 4; Eldred G. Smith, Discourse delivered March 10, 1964, at Brigham Young University, in *BYU Speeches of the Year* (1964), 8; Gordon B. Hinckley, *Teachings of Gordon B. Hinckley* (Salt Lake City, UT: Deseret Book, 1997), 147; David O. McKay, "An Address on the Temple Ceremony," given to missionaries at the Salt Lake Temple Annex, Thursday, September 25, 1941, Harold B. Lee Library, Special Collections, Brigham Young University, 2–3; James E. Talmage, *The House of the Lord* (Salt Lake City, UT: The Church of Jesus Christ of Latter-day Saints, 2013), 88; Jeffrey R. Holland, "Keeping Covenants: A Message for Those Who Will Serve a Mission," in *New Era*, January 2012, 4; Robert D. Hales, "The Aaronic Priesthood: Return with Honor," in *Ensign*, May 1990, 39; Ezra Taft Benson, "A Vision and a Hope for the Youth of Zion," in *Brigham Young University, Speeches of the Year*, April 12, 1977, BYU Devotional, 1. See also Hugh Nibley, *Approaching Zion* (Provo/Salt Lake City, UT: Foundation for Ancient Research and Mormon Studies/Deseret Book, 1989), 441–2; Immo Luschin, "Latter-day Saint Temple Worship and Activity, in *Encyclopedia of Mormonism*, Daniel H. Ludlow, ed., four volumes (New York: Macmillan, 1994), 4:1447; Alma P. Burton, "Endowment," in Ludlow (1994), 2:455; Jeffrey M. Bradshaw, "The Five Celestial Laws," in Jeffery M. Bradshaw, *Temple Themes in the Book of Moses* (Salt Lake City, UT: Eborn Books, 2010), 203–216.

3. Boyd K. Packer, *Our Father's Plan*, rev. ed. (Salt Lake City: Deseret Book, 1994), 46, emphasis added.

4. Hugh Nibley, *Eloquent Witness: Nibley on Himself, Others, and the Temple* (Provo, UT: Foundation for Ancient Research and Mormon Studies, 2008), 329–30.

5. Ezra Taft Benson, *The Teachings of Ezra Taft Benson* (Salt Lake City, UT: Bookcraft, 1998), 251–52, emphasis added.

6. Boyd K. Packer, *The Holy Temple* (Salt Lake City, UT: Bookcraft, 1980), 30.

7. "So You Are Going To The Temple," Joseph Fieldling Smith, Harold B. Lee, and N. Eldon Tanner, circular letter, February 12, 1971, 1.

❦ *53* ❦

What is a "living ordinance"?

A "living ordinance" is one that is performed for someone who is alive, rather than for someone who is deceased. For example, in the Church we have *baptism* and also *baptism for the dead*. Baptism is what we do for a living eight-year-old or for a convert to the Church. Baptism for the dead is what we do in the temple for someone who, when they died, was not yet a member of the Church. Thus, baptism for the dead is not called a "living ordinance," whereas convert baptisms are.

When you go to the temple to participate in your first initiatory and endowment ceremonies, those would be "living ordinances" because they are being performed specifically for *you*—a living person. After you have received your own endowment, each time you go back to the temple to participate in an initiatory/endowment, you will be performing those ordinances for someone who is deceased and, thus, those would not be "living ordinances."

This same principle applies to temple sealings. When you go to the temple to be sealed to your spouse or your children, those are "living ordinances." If you go to perform those same ceremonies on behalf of someone who is deceased, they would not be "living ordinances."

The vast majority of work you will do in the temple during your lifetime will *not* be living ordinances. It will instead be sacred work for the dead.

54

What are the "prayer roll" and the "prayer circle"?

The "prayer roll" is a list of names of people who have serious needs in their lives and could be blessed by the prayers of the faithful on their behalf. Each of the temples keeps a list of these names, which members of the Church have submitted, and then—during each endowment ceremony—the various people in attendance exercise their faith in support of those persons whose names are written on the temple prayer roll, as a prayer is offered on their behalf. One can submit their own name or the name of someone else in need by either going to the temple and writing those names on the prayer roll or by calling any temple of The Church of Jesus Christ of Latter-day Saints and asking them to write the name of a person in need on the roll.

In his book *The Holy Temple*, President Boyd K. Packer (1924–2015)—former President of the Quorum of the Twelve Apostles—spoke of members of the Church "dressed in the proper way for temple ordinance work," approaching "the altar in the true order of prayer."[1] Regarding the "prayer circle" and "the true order of prayer," the *Encyclopedia of Mormonism* explains, "The prayer circle is a part of Latter-day Saint temple worship, usually associated with the Endowment ceremony. Participants, an equal number of men and women dressed in temple clothing, surround an altar in a circle formation to participate unitedly in prayer."[2]

It was apparently somewhat common for early Christians to participate in these prayer circles, where one person said the prayer and others repeated the words of the prayer (as a means of showing that they agreed with what was being prayed). We have, for example, an early text known as the *Acts of John*[3] in which we are told that Jesus "assembled [His disciples] and said, 'Before I am delivered to them [who seek my death], let us [pray] to the Father . . .'[4] So he told [the Apostles] to form a circle, holding one another's hands, and he himself stood in the middle and said, 'Answer Amen to me.'" In other words, after Jesus would say a phrase as part of His prayer, He wanted His disciples to say "Amen," implying that they agreed with that part of the prayer, as though they had said it themselves.[5] This ancient text continues: "So he [meaning Jesus] began to . . . say, 'Glory be to thee, Father.' And we [apostles] circled round him and answered him, 'Amen' [after each thing he said] . . ."[6]

Of the symbolism of prayer circles, the *Encyclopedia of Mormonism* goes on to explain:

> The circle is an ancient and universal symbol of perfection . . . The formation of the prayer circle suggests wholeness and eternity, and the participants, having affirmed that they bear no negative feelings toward other members of the circle (cf. Matt. 5:23–24), evoke communal harmony in collective prayer—a harmony underscored by the linked formation, uniformity of dress, and the unison repetition of the words of the leader. The prayer has no set text, but is, among other things, an occasion for seeking the Lord's blessing upon those with particular needs whose names have been submitted for collective entreaty.[7]

Another source notes: "In forming the prayer circle one excludes the outer world." The participants "form closed circles with their backs all turned on the outer world."[8] The altar being their focus, symbolically speaking, the participants are concentrating on the sacrifice of Christ (represented by the altar), while forgetting or rejecting the world (to which they have turned their backs).

Each time you attend an endowment ceremony in the temple, you will have the opportunity to participate in a prayer circle and exercise your faith on behalf of the people whose names are written on the prayer roll of that temple.

Notes

1. Boyd K. Packer, *The Holy Temple* (Salt Lake City, UT: Bookcraft, 1980), 3–4.

2. George S. Tate, "Prayer Circle," in *Encyclopedia of Mormonism*, Daniel H. Ludlow, ed., four volumes (New York: Macmillan, 1994), 3:1120. See also, Andrew F. Ehat and Lyndon W. Cook, *The Words of Joseph Smith* (Provo, UT: Religious Studies Center, Brigham Young University, 1980), 53–54, note 19.

3. This ancient pseudepigraphical text—most likely Gnostic in origin—was certainly known in the Christian Church by the fourth century. See Edgar Hennecke and Wilhelm Schneemelcher, ed., *New Testament Apocrypha*, volume two (Philadelphia: The Westminster Press, 1965), 192. Since Clement of Alexandria (AD 150–215) makes reference to it, it is likely that the *Acts of John* should be dated as early as the second century AD. See Frederick W. Norris, "Acts of John," in Everett Ferguson, editor, *Encyclopedia of Early Christianity* (New York: Garland Publishing, 1990), 7.

4. Nibley noted: "The prayer circle is often called the *chorus* of the apostles, and it is the meaning of *chorus* which can be a choir, but is originally a ring dance . . ." [Hugh Nibley, *Mormonism and Early Christianity* (Provo, UT: Foundation for Ancient Research and Mormon Studies, 1987), 53]. It is a hymn, of sorts, unto God, offered in the Spirit of D&C 25:12—"For my soul delighteth in the song of the heart; yea, the song of the righteous is a prayer unto me, and it shall be answered with a blessing upon their heads." Thus, the prayer is as a hymn, which invokes God's choicest blessings upon those who participate.

5. Nibley wrote: "The prayer spoken in the circle differs every time; it is not strictly prescribed. The one leading the prayer expresses himself as the Spirit moves him, and the others either repeat each line after him (which would not be necessary if they all knew it by heart) or add an 'amen' at the end of each phrase, which is the equivalent of reciting the prayer for oneself." Hugh Nibley, *Mormonism and Early Christianity* (Provo, UT: Foundation for Ancient Research and Mormon Studies, 1987), 56.

6. Acts of John 94–97, in Edgar Hennecke and Wilhelm Schneemelcher, ed., *New Testament Apocrypha*, volume two (Philadelphia: The Westminster Press, 1965), 227–228 & 232.

7. George S. Tate, "Prayer Circle," in *Encyclopedia of Mormonism*, Daniel H. Ludlow, ed., four volumes (New York: Macmillan, 1994), 3:1120.

8. Hugh Nibley, *Mormonism and Early Christianity* (Provo, UT: Foundation for Ancient Research and Mormon Studies, 1987), 70.

55

Do all temples show a movie as part of the endowment?

No. While most temples have a video presentation as part of the endowment, the Salt Lake and Manti temples currently do not. In those older temples, ordinance workers tell (or act out) the story of the Creation and the Fall. The *Encyclopedia of Mormonism* explains, "In the older temples, larger rooms are decorated to represent the Creation, the Garden of Eden, this world, and the terrestrial kingdom, and in such endowment rooms, participants watch and hear figurative presentations in which scenes are acted out, depicting by whom and why the earth was created and how one may come to dwell again in God's presence."[1]

One of the advantages the film has over using live actors has to do with patrons who speak a foreign language. The temples that use live actors to tell the story of the Creation and Fall can only present the endowment in one language at a time. However, in temples that use a video presentation, special headsets are given to those patrons who speak a language other than the one the film is being shown in. Consequently, with the video presentation, the endowment can be presented in several languages in the same room at the same time.

Note

1. Immo Luschin, "Latter-day Saint Temple Worship and Activity," in *Encyclopedia of Mormonism*, Daniel H. Ludlow, ed., four volumes (New York: Macmillan, 1994), 4:1447.

56

Is it true that men and women sit separately during the endowment?

Yes, it is true that during the endowment ceremony, men and women are seated on opposite sides of the same room. This is not designed to segregate but instead functions as a great teaching tool.

Throughout the various stages of the endowment—which represent the Creation, the Fall, the post-Fall telestial world, and the terrestrial (or millennial) earth—men and women are seated separately. Only in the celestial room and sealing rooms do we see men and women mingling. This reminds us of the eternal truth that *only in exaltation*, the highest degree of glory in the celestial kingdom, will we be united as husbands and wives and as eternal families. Thus, as we sit separately during the endowment and as we are taught about the various stages of the plan of salvation, we are constantly reminded of the need to enter into sacred covenants that will bind our spouse and our children to us for time and for all eternity. Being seated separately functions well as an invitation to be sealed as a family and to live faithful to our covenants so that we can be together—not separate—*forever!*

57

I hear that there is a bunch of stuff you have to remember in the temple. What if I'm not very good at memorizing?

While you are taught many things in the temple, particularly during the endowment, there is actually very little that you *have to* memorize. As explained in Question #32, there is a "new name" that you should commit to memory. However, if you forget it, the temple can remind you of what that name was.

The remainder of the things you will be told, you do not *have to* memorize. There is a point in the endowment at which you are asked about a few of the things you were taught in the temple that day.[1] However, if you do not have these things memorized, you need not worry. There will *always* be an ordinance worker standing right next to you that will prompt you with *anything* you can't remember. Thus, there is no stress about needing to memorize things in the temple.

Actually, as you attend the temple regularly, you'll find that much of the ceremony will become so familiar to you that even if you do struggle to memorize things you will start to know the ceremony by heart—simply from participating in it regularly.

Note

1. John A. Widtsoe, *A Rational Theology*, 7th ed. (Salt Lake City, UT: Deseret Book, 1966), 125-126; Brigham Young, discourse given May 24, 1863, in *Journal of Discourses*, 10:172; Brigham Young, discourse given August 8, 1844, Nauvoo, IL, in *The Complete Discourses of Brigham Young*, five volumes, Richard S. Van Wagoner, ed. (Salt Lake City, UT: The Smith-Pettit Foundation, 1999), 1:43; Brigham Young, discourse given April 6, 1853, in *Journal of Discourses* 2:31;

David O. McKay, "An Address on the Temple Ceremony," given to missionaries at the Salt Lake Temple Annex, Thursday, September 25, 1941. Harold B. Lee Library, Special Collections, Brigham Young University, 3; Boyd K. Packer, *Our Father's Plan*, rev. ed. (Salt Lake City: Deseret Book, 1994), 46; John A Widtsoe, "Symbolism in the Temple," in *Saviors on Mount Zion*, ed. Archibald F. Bennett (Salt Lake City: Deseret Sunday School Union Board, 1950), 166; Todd Compton, "Symbolism," in *Encyclopedia of Mormonism*, Daniel H. Ludlow, ed., four volumes (New York: Macmillan, 1994), 3:1430; Ed J. Pinegar, *The Temple: Gaining Knowledge and Power in the House of the Lord* (American Fork, UT: Covenant Communications, 2014), 223.

58

I've heard that there is a temple "veil"—kind of like those in ancient temples. What is that about?

Yes, that is true. As noted, ancient Jewish temples had a veil that separated the Holy Place from the Holy of Holies (see Exodus 26:31–35; Matthew 27:51). Latter-day Saint temples have something very similar. The *Encyclopedia of Mormonism* explains, "A veil symbolically divides the terrestrial room from the celestial room" of the temple.[1]

Figuratively, this veil reminds us that in our fallen mortal state we are separated from God our Father and Jesus our Savior. At the end of the endowment ceremony, you will symbolically act out the judgment day[2] and then pass through the veil of the temple. This passing through the veil symbolizes our eventual return to God at the end of our mortal lives.[3]

Notes

1. Immo Luschin, "Latter-day Saint Temple Worship and Activity, in *Encyclopedia of Mormonism*, Daniel H. Ludlow, ed., four volumes (New York: Macmillan, 1994), 4:1447.
2. See Boyd K. Packer, *Our Father's Plan*, rev. ed. (Salt Lake City: Deseret Book, 1994), 46; Brigham Young, discourse given May 24, 1863, in *Journal of Discourses*, 10:172; Brigham Young, discourse given August 8, 1844, Nauvoo, IL, in *The Complete Discourses of Brigham Young*, five volumes, Richard S. Van Wagoner, ed. (Salt Lake City, UT: The Smith-Pettit Foundation, 1999), 1:43; Brigham Young, discourse given April 6, 1853, in *Journal of Discourses* 2:31; John A Widtsoe, "Symbolism in the Temple," in *Saviors on Mount Zion*, ed. Archibald F. Bennett (Salt Lake City: Deseret Sunday School Union Board, 1950), 166; John A. Widtsoe, *A Rational Theology*, 7th ed. (Salt Lake City: Deseret Book, 1966), 125–26. To have a better understanding of this symbolic ritual at the end of the

endowment, you may wish to read my article "Grace at the Veil" in Alonzo L. Gaskill, *Temple Reflections: Insights into the House of the Lord* (Springville, UT: Cedar Fort, 2016), 25–35.

3. See Todd Compton, "Symbolism," in *Encyclopedia of Mormonism*, Daniel H. Ludlow, ed., four volumes (New York: Macmillan, 1994), 3:1430.

59

I've heard that some of the language in the temple feels a bit patriarchal. Is that accurate?

The world and its various cultures are constantly in flux. Things change unceasingly. Modern views of women, for example, are much different than ancient views espoused by more patriarchal societies. For example, in biblical times the inability to bear children was typically seen as a curse from God, as a sign of sinfulness, or as evidence that the childless woman was rejected by the divine[1] (e.g., Genesis 11:30, 25:21, 29:31; 1 Samuel 1; Proverbs 30:16; Luke 1:25, etc.). Today, however, members of the Church would *absolutely* reject that explanation of barrenness. Similarly, in 1 Corinthians 14, the Apostle Paul counseled the women of Corinth to "keep silent" in church, for it was "a shame for women to speak in the church" (vv. 34–35). While there were cultural things going on in Corinth at the time that were likely behind Paul's counsel to *those specific Saints*, nevertheless, some religions today take this as a commandment that should be obeyed by all Christian denominations in the modern era.[2] However, in The Church of Jesus Christ of Latter-day Saints, we would *not* see this as an applicable rule in our dispensation. Rather than saying that sisters should be silent in church, today we teach that it is imperative that they speak—and that their voices are heard.[3] These are but two of many potential examples showing how the culture of past eras was very patriarchal.

As mentioned in Question #5, the way in which the ordinances of the temple have been performed in each dispensation has also varied—contingent upon the needs of the members and the culture of a given era. The Prophet Joseph Smith (1805–1844) restored a series of *ancient* ordinances and rites associated with temple worship. The language of the temple—both anciently and today—is highly symbolic. When those antique rites were first restored (through the Prophet), they were largely clothed in the *ancient* symbols from a previous dispensation. Some of those *ancient* rites—when first restored—naturally felt patriarchal to some, as their symbols were foreign to our modern culture and contemporary way of communicating truths. President David O. McKay (1873–1970), ninth President of the Church, noted that he had met some who had been bothered by such things. He said, "I have analyzed" their concerns and "I have listened to them, and I have come to the conclusion that in nearly every case" the person who was bothered by something they heard or saw done during the ordinances "has failed to comprehend the significance of the message that is given in the temple." Then President McKay added, "[they] have become absorbed in what I am going to call the 'mechanics' of the Temple and, while criticizing these, they have failed to get the *spiritual* significance."[4] President McKay was not being critical of those who struggled to see a positive meaning in some of the ancient symbols. Rather, he was simply suggesting that the symbols themselves sometimes caused people to miss the spiritual significance of what the endowment was designed to teach. Because many of those *ancient* symbols sometimes served as a distraction, in the years since God began to reveal these sacred ordinances to Joseph Smith, many modernizations have taken place. Indeed, as noted earlier, on January 2, 2019, the First Presidency of the Church released a statement in which they explained, "Details associated with temple work have been adjusted periodically, including language, methods of construction, communication, and record-keeping. Prophets have taught that there will be no end to such adjustments as directed by the Lord to His servants."[5] President Russell M. Nelson (b. 1924) likewise recently wrote:

Year by year and step by step, revelation has come to successive prophets. President Wilford Woodruff taught this concept when speaking in general conference in April 1894: "[Joseph Smith and Brigham Young] did not receive all the revelations that belong to [temple] work; neither did President Taylor, nor has Wilford Woodruff. There will be no end to this work until it is perfected.[6]

Those *ancient* rites that appeared patriarchal (when first restored) have been modernized in our dispensation to fit the culture and doctrinal understandings that we have in the dispensation of the fullness of times (Ephesians 1:10). Both men and women should be pleased with how God has guided His modern prophets and apostles to improve the rites and ordinances of the past, making them more meaningful and applicable to those living in our dispensation.

Notes

1. See, for example, Leland Ryken, James C. Wilohit, and Tremper Longman III, ed., *Dictionary of Biblical Imagery* (Downers Grove, IL: InterVarsity Press, 1998), 75.

2. See, for example, Watch Tower Bible and Tract Society of Pennsylvania, *Insight On The Scriptures*, two volumes (Brooklyn, New York; Watchtower Bible and Tract Society of New York, 1988), 2:1197.

3. See, for example, M. Russell Ballard, *Counseling with our Counsels*, revised edition (Salt Lake City, UT: Deseret Book, 2012), 55–62; Dale G. Renlund and Ruth L. Renlund, *The Melchizedek Priesthood: Understanding the Doctrine—Living the Principles* (Salt Lake City, UT: Deseret Book, 2018), 142–143.

4. David O. McKay, "An Address on the Temple Ceremony," given to missionaries at the Salt Lake Temple Annex, Thursday, September 25, 1941. Harold B. Lee Library, Special Collections, Brigham Young University, 1.

5. See "First Presidency Statement on Temples," January 2, 2019, https://www.mormonnewsroom.org/article/temple-worship.

6. Russell M. Nelson, *Accomplishing the Impossible: What God Does—What We Can Do* (Salt Lake City, UT: Deseret Book, 2015), 63, bracketed insertions present in the original quotation.

60

How will I know which things are important to focus on and which are not?

Perhaps one of the biggest mistakes people make when they receive their own endowment is that they stress about remembering everything they are told in a nearly two-hour ceremony. This is *not* the best approach to your first time in an endowment ceremony. You will have a lifetime to attend the temple and learn what the Lord is trying to teach you there. I have been attending regularly for decades, and I continue to see and learn new things in the temple. Thus, you are not going to grasp all of the details on your first, tenth, or even hundredth time in the temple. It will take a lifetime to see, hear, and know what it is the Lord is trying to say to *you* through these sacred ceremonies. Indeed, that is one of the beauties of the temple. You can go thousands of times and, because of the symbolism, continue to learn new things from the same ordinances that you've seen performed over and over again.

So if it isn't possible to take in everything during your first endowment ceremony, and if trying to do so would be more distracting than helpful, then what *should* you focus on during that first visit? Well, various people will have differing opinions about this. Here are a few suggestions.

First, you will make several covenants during your endowment (see Question #45). These are sacred promises to God that, if you are faithful to them, will bring you tremendous blessings—in this life and in the life to come. As you make each of those covenants, I would encourage you to think about those and perhaps ask yourself, "Am I fully committed to keeping this covenant with God?" Making covenants is perhaps the most important thing you will do during your endowment. It is worth thinking about those promises as you make them and after you leave the temple.

Second, I think it is always helpful when you are in the temple to look for things that remind you of Christ. Jesus is at the heart of *all that we do* in the temple. It is because of His atoning sacrifice that what we do therein matters. A significant portion of temple symbolism is about Him. Consequently, if you look for symbols of Him, that will help you to both feel the Holy Ghost and understand the most sacred part of temple worship.

Third, many people are counseled to pay attention to the spirit of peace that is present in the temple. If you get too caught up in the little details—and all of the things that might have meaning that you are potentially missing—you run the risk of not noticing the spirit of calm and peace that is available to us in the house of the Lord. Do not, on your first experience with the endowment, let yourself get so distracted by the many small and curious details that you miss that spirit of peace.

Fourth, there is some benefit in making a mental note of things you have questions about as you participate in the endowment. When you are in the celestial room, at the conclusion of the ceremony, you will have the opportunity to ask those questions of your family and friends who were in attendance with you. While they may know some of the answers to your questions, they also may not. Thus, you should remember that it is your responsibility to study and try to prayerfully find answers to the questions you may have had as you attended the temple.

Those are a few suggestions of things you might wish to focus on. As you prepare to attend the temple for the first time, you may wish to ask your bishop (branch president), stake (or mission) president, parent, or close friend what *they* would suggest you focus on during your first experience with the endowment ceremony. As you glean a few of these suggestions, prayerfully ask your Father in Heaven which of these would be most beneficial to *you*, and then follow His counsel. The many other suggestions made to you in this book, and by others you've asked, can be beneficial on future visits to the temple.

61

When someone says they are going to the temple to "do a session," what does that mean?

"Do a session" is kind of *Mormon slang* for participating in an endowment ceremony at the temple. While it is common to use language like this, it may be best to avoid such casual descriptions of the sacred work that takes place in the house of the Lord. Speaking more reverently about what we do in the temple increases the likelihood that we will feel the Spirit in association with the work we perform there. Also, speaking in reverent tones about temple work will help our children and grandchildren to sense how sacred the temple is, and our non-LDS acquaintances will be more likely to feel drawn to the house of the Lord when we speak of it in hallowed ways.

Instead of saying that you are going to "do a session" at the temple, you might instead say you are going to the temple to "participate in an endowment session," to "redeem the dead," or to "worship your Father in Heaven." The wording is subtly different from "doing a session," but the slight difference shows a bit more reverence for the sacred work we do within God's holy house.

The Sealing Ordinances

62

What do I need to bring with me to my sealing?

On the day that you are sealed in the temple, you will need to take with you to the temple several things.

First of all, if you're able, take with you someone you are close to—someone who is the same gender as you, has already received his or her endowment, and can serve as your escort in the temple that day.

Second, you will need to bring with you your temple recommend and also a recommend for living ordinances (see Question #11). Your bishop will issue those to you, and both your bishop and stake president will sign them for you. Because you will need an interview with both your bishop (or branch president) and stake (or mission) president to get these two recommends, you'll want to set appointments for those interviews several weeks before you plan on being sealed. You should call their executive secretaries to schedule those appointments.

Third—if you are *not* already legally married to the person you are being sealed to—in many countries you will need to bring with you to the temple a state-issued marriage license. For example, if you are getting sealed in the Salt Lake Temple, you would need to bring with you a marriage license issued in the state of Utah within thirty days of when you will be sealed. If you are already married but are now simply being sealed, you will not need to bring a marriage license with you to your sealing. (It is best to contact the temple you will be sealed in to ascertain the laws for the area of the world in which you will be sealed.)

Fourth, special clothing is worn in the temple by those partici-pating in the sealing ordinance (see Question #43). Some temples will have clothing you can rent, but others may not. If the temple you will be sealed in does not have a clothing rental, you may need to bring your own temple clothes. Well before the day of your sealing, call the temple you plan on being sealed in and ask them if they have clothing rental services. If they do not, an endowed family member or your bishop or Relief Society president can help you to get the clothing you will need for that special day.

Finally, for your sealing, you will need two witnesses to the ordinance. Some couples like to have their fathers serve as the wit-nesses for their sealing, though you may select any worthy male who holds a current temple recommend and the Melchizedek Priesthood and who has already received his endowment in the temple.

63

What covenants will I make
when I am sealed?

The covenants made in the sealing ordinance are largely encapsulated in *The Family: A Proclamation to the World*.[1] Before being sealed, it would be wise for you and those to whom you will be sealed to study this inspired document and contemplate what it is that the Lord is asking you to do and to be. Each of the principles taught in that divinely revealed proclamation are foundational to the temple sealing ordinances. Among other things, the sealing ordinance (for marriage) highlights the fact that husbands and wives "have a solemn responsibility to love and care for each other" (paragraph 6). The following declaration, found in the proclamation, is also central to the covenants made during the sealing ceremony: "By divine design, fathers are to preside over their families in love and righteousness and are responsible to provide the necessities of life and protection for their families. Mothers are primarily responsible for the nurture of their children. In these sacred responsibilities, fathers and mothers are obligated to help one another as equal partners" (paragraph 7). In addition, we are reminded in the *Proclamation* and in the sealing ceremony that "God's commandment for His children to multiply and replenish the earth remains in force" and that He "has commanded that the sacred powers of procreation are to be employed only between man and woman, lawfully wedded as husband and wife" (paragraph 4).

One of the most important covenants you will make when you are sealed "for time and for all eternity" is to seek to become one—something the Lord repeatedly commands of husbands and wives (see Genesis 2:24; Matthew 19:15–16; Mark 10:8; D&C 49:16;

Moses 3:24; Abraham 5:18; 1 Corinthians 6:16; Ephesians 5:31; D&C 38:27). The marriage wherein the husband and wife do not strive consistently to become one is the marriage that is at grave risk of failing.

Elder Orson Pratt (1811–1881), of the Quorum of the Twelve Apostles, described in detail the temple sealing ceremony of his day (see Question #5) in the Church's official publication, *The Latter-day Saints' Millennial Star.*[2] In that periodical, Elder Pratt said that couples being sealed "for time and for all eternity" make a covenant to "receive" each other, and to "fulfill all [of] the laws, rites, and ordinances, pertaining to holy matrimony, in the new and everlasting covenant"—including the commandment to "be fruitful and multiply, and replenish the earth."[3] Consequently, in Elder Pratt's view, one might summarize some of the covenants you will make when you are sealed as follows:

+ *Receiving:* According to Elder Pratt, when sealed, you covenant that you will *receive* your spouse—somewhat like Paul suggested when he wrote, "Let the husband render unto the wife due benevolence: and likewise also the wife unto the husband. The wife hath not power of her own body, but the husband: and likewise also the husband hath not power of his own body, but the wife" (1 Corinthians 7:3–4; see also Ephesians 5:25, 28 & 33). According to Paul's perspective, once we are married, we live for our partners—and not for ourselves. We give freely of ourselves and receive our spouses freely, that we two may become one (Ephesians 5:31; see also Genesis 2:24; Matthew 19:5–6). You are to give yourself and to receive your spouse—emotionally, spiritually, intellectually, physically, and intimately.[4] Ultimately, your covenant implies that you will be available to your eternal mate in every sense and in every way, assuming that the two of you are living as your covenants suggest that you should.[5]

+ *Multiply and Replenish:* Elder Pratt indicated that, when sealed, you covenant that, if biologically capable, the two of you will seek to multiply and replenish the earth. Certainly this fulfills God's plan to send children down into families who are bound by sacred and eternal covenants. Elder Pratt taught that we also multiply and replenish the earth so that we "may have joy and rejoicing in [our] posterity."[6] One of the great joys of mortality is to have children and to experience the happiness (and challenges) of raising them up unto the Lord.

♦ *Obey the New and Everlasting Covenant:* Finally, Elder Pratt suggested that when you are sealed, you covenant that you will keep all of the "laws, rites, and ordinances" associated with the "new and everlasting covenant"[7]—which is the restored gospel of Jesus Christ. Thus, when you are sealed, you are promising to live a fully consecrated and faithful life; doing all within your power to keep the various covenants and duties associated with eternal marriage and the restored gospel—including any commandment or law pertaining to marriage and family life.

Elder Pratt went on to explain that faithfulness to these covenants (associated with the sealing ordinance) would bring upon the couple sealed the promise that "all that [the] Father hath shall be given unto" them (D&C 84:38).[8]

The ordinance that seals husbands and wives together for eternity speaks unequivocally about the unity which *must* exist if the couple is to achieve happiness in this life, and exaltation in the next. Elder Jeffrey R. Holland emphasized this eternal truth when he taught, "Marriage was intended to mean the complete merger of a man and a woman—their hearts, hopes, lives, love, family, future, everything. . . . This is a union of such completeness that we use the word *seal* to convey its eternal promise."[9] In anticipation of your sealing, perhaps one of the best questions you could ask yourself would be "Is the person I am getting sealed to someone whom I can live unitedly with *in every facet* of my life? Can I achieve, with him or her, the 'completeness' Elder Holland spoke of?" If your answer is "no," then perhaps moving forward with this specific person should be reconsidered. After all, as noted earlier (see Question #1), the ultimate purpose of temples is the exaltation of families. As President Russell M. Nelson (b. 1924) has stated, "This Church was restored so that families could be formed, sealed, and exalted eternally." President Nelson added, "While salvation is an individual matter, exaltation is a family matter."[10] And that requires *unity*. President Ezra Taft Benson (1899–1994), thirteenth

President of the Church, similarly taught, "The temple is an ever-present reminder that God intends the family to be eternal."[11] Elder Bruce R. McConkie (1915–1985), of the Quorum of the Twelve Apostles, likewise explained: "The great work of every man"—and he could just as well have said *woman*—is "to create and perfect an eternal family unit."[12] And Sister Julie B. Beck (b. 1954), former Relief Society general president, taught: "When we speak of qualifying for the blessings of eternal life, we mean qualifying for the blessings of eternal families."[13] The sealing ceremony, and the covenants associated with it, strongly emphasize this foundational eternal truth. Perhaps this is why the sealing ordinance has been referred to as the temple's "crowning blessing."[14]

Notes

1. "The Family: A Proclamation to the World," *Ensign,* November 2010, 129.

2. Orson Pratt, "Celestial Marriage in Deseret," in *The Latter-day Saints' Millennial Star,* No. 14, Vol. XV (Saturday, April 2, 1853): 214–215. See also Orson Pratt, *The Seer,* photo-reprint of original (Salt Lake City, UT: Eborn Books, 2000), 31–32.

3. See Orson Pratt, "Celestial Marriage in Deseret," in *The Latter-day Saints' Millennial Star,* No. 14, Vol. XV (Saturday, April 2, 1853): 215.

4. Speaking of the entire set of ordinances and covenants received in the temple, Ed J. Pinegar wrote about what he called "The Doctrine of Receiving." See Ed J. Pinegar, *The Temple: Gaining Knowledge and Power in the House of the Lord* (American Fork, UT: Covenant Communications, 2014), 181–183.

5. In other words, your covenant does *not* ask you to tolerate abuse by an unrighteous partner.

6. Orson Pratt, "Celestial Marriage in Deseret," in *The Latter-day Saints' Millennial Star,* No. 14, Vol. XV (Saturday, April 2, 1853): 215.

7. Orson Pratt, "Celestial Marriage in Deseret," in *The Latter-day Saints' Millennial Star,* No. 14, Vol. XV (Saturday, April 2, 1853): 215.

8. See Orson Pratt, "Celestial Marriage in Deseret," in *The Latter-day Saints' Millennial Star,* No. 14, Vol. XV (Saturday, April 2, 1853): 215. See also Orson Pratt, in *Journal of Discourses* 1:294, 2:102, 8:106 & 17:153.

9. Jeffrey R. Holland, "Personal Purity," in *Ensign,* November 1998, 76.

10. Russell M. Nelson, *Hope in Our Hearts* (Salt Lake City, UT: Deseret Book, 2009), 36, 35 and 34.

11. Ezra Taft Benson, *The Teachings of Ezra Taft Benson* (Salt Lake City, UT: Bookcraft, 1998), 538.

12. Bruce R. McConkie, in *Conference Report,* April 1970, 27. See also Henry B. Eyring, "Eternal Families," in *Ensign,* May 2016, 81.

13. Julie B. Beck, "Teaching the Doctrine of the Family," in *Ensign,* March 2011, 13.

14. Boyd K. Packer, *The Holy Temple* (Salt Lake City, UT: Bookcraft, 1980), 8.

64

If I have received my endowment but have not yet been sealed to a spouse, can I watch or participate in temple sealings?

Yes, if you have already received your endowment in the temple, and if you worthily hold a current temple recommend, you are authorized to witness the sealing of someone who has invited you to be in attendance at his or her sealing ceremony. In addition, you may participate in sealings for the dead, if you have already received your temple endowment but are not yet sealed to a spouse.

{65}

If I recently got married civilly, how long must I wait before I can be sealed in the temple?

If you and your spouse were both members of the Church at the time you were married civilly, you will typically have to wait one year (from the date of your civil marriage) before you can be sealed in the temple.

However, there are a few exceptions to this rule. For example, a couple living in a country that requires civil marriages (because it doesn't recognize temple sealings as valid) would not necessarily have to wait a year after their civil marriage to be sealed. Also, a couple living in a country where there is no temple, and where the country in which they live does not acknowledge marriages performed outside of the country, may not have to wait a year after their civil marriage in order to be sealed in the temple. (In both of these cases, the couple should seek to receive their endowment and be sealed in the temple as soon after their civil marriage as is feasible.) In addition, the current Church policy allows couples in which one or both have been members less than a year at the time they were married to receive their endowment and be sealed any time after the passing of the one-year anniversary of their confirmation as members of the Church.

66

What should I wear to my own temple sealing? And what should I wear to the sealing of a friend or family member?

When you are sealed in the temple, you will dress in white clothing over which you will wear the "the robes of the Holy Priesthood."[1] Some brides have desired to be sealed while wearing their wedding dress, with a long train on the back, and with their wedding veil and high heels on. While such clothing—assuming it is modest—would typically be appropriately worn outside of the temple when taking wedding photos, such clothing is secular and is best not worn during one's sealing. Instead, the groom traditionally would wear a white shirt, pants, and tie with his temple robes worn on top of those items. A bride would normally wear a modest white temple dress with her temple robes worn on top. (It is worth noting, if a bride arrives at the temple with a dress that is sheer, low-cut, or in some other way immodest or revealing, the temple will typically require that she either wear a camisole—or the equivalent—underneath the dress or wear a temple dress provided by the temple instead of the dress she has brought. Thus, it is imperative that brides select attire that is appropriate for the house of the Lord.) After the bride and groom have been sealed, and before exiting the temple, they will have the opportunity to change into their formal wedding attire (if they have brought formal wear) so that those awaiting their exit from the temple will see them in whatever finery they have chosen to wear.

As we noted in Question #16 above, President Russell M. Nelson (b. 1924), seventeenth President of the Church, has said,

"One prepares physically for the temple by dressing properly. It is not a place for casual attire."[2] If you have received your endowment and will be attending the sealing of a friend or family member, you should wear what we've come to call our "Sunday best." In other words, you should dress in the type of attire that you might wear to Church. The clothing you wear to the temple should be clean, modest, and non-distracting. It should be of such a nature that it shows your reverence for the Lord and for the sacred ordinance that you will be witnessing that day.

Notes

1. See "Sacred Temple Clothing," found at the official website of The Church of Jesus Christ of Latter-day Saints (https://www.lds.org/media-library/video/2014-01-1460-sacred-temple-clothing?lang=eng#d), © 2015 by Intellectual Reserve, Inc.
2. Russell M. Nelson, *Hope in Our Hearts* (Salt Lake City, UT: Deseret Book, 2009), 105.

67

Who decides who serves as the "witnesses" for a temple sealing?

You get to choose who serves as the two witnesses for your temple sealing. Of course, each of the witnesses must hold a current temple recommend, be worthy of that recommend, hold the Melchizedek Priesthood, and have previously received his own endowment. If they qualify in each of those areas, you may invite them to serve as one of the two official witnesses to your sealing.

In my own case, because neither my father nor my wife's father were members of the Church, we selected a current bishop and a past bishop—whom we dearly loved—to serve as our witnesses. Similarly, on a number of occasions, I have had the privilege of serving as the witness for dear friends who were being sealed for time and for all eternity.

This is your sealing and your special day. Based on the standards explained above, it will be your opportunity to select those whom *you* would most want to be a witness to your temple sealing.

{68}

Whom should I invite to my sealing?

Your own sealing is a once-in-a-lifetime event and, thus, many agonize over whom they should invite. There are a couple of factors to consider in creating your guest list.

First, remember that a temple sealing is a sacred ordinance. Those invited to attend must have received their own temple endowment and should be faithfully keeping the commandments. While it may be tempting to invite someone who is close to you but who is not currently keeping his or her covenants, such would be inappropriate. Doing so would hinder the Spirit that should be present in such a sacred setting, and it would mock both the ordinance and Heavenly Father. We must keep His house and his ordinances sacred. Thus, we should only invite those who are truly worthy to be there.

Second, while you can invite as many guests as you would like to your reception, by design, space is limited in temple sealing rooms (see Question #41). If the number of people in attendance is excessive, one runs the risk of losing the spirit of holiness that should prevail during a sealing and, instead, creating an atmosphere that would be more appropriate at a reception, rather than at a temple sealing. Thus, the sealing rooms in temples are designed to be large enough for one's immediate family but small enough to prevent an excessive number of guests that might provoke a spirit of irreverence. Consequently, in creating a guest list for your sealing, it is best to invite those who are closest to you. One need not fill every seat in the sealing room. Only invite those who will add to the spirit of reverence and who will sense the sacred nature of what is happening on that holy occasion.[1]

Though it doesn't happen often, sometimes individuals will request that a favorite general authority perform their sealing, thinking that this will somehow make the ceremony more special. President Boyd K. Packer (1924–2015), former President of the Quorum of the Twelve Apostles, indicated that the First Presidency has asked that members not make such requests of General Authorities. If General Authorities accepted all of the invitations they receive to seal couples and families, they would be unable to tend to their very heavy and sacred responsibilities—responsibilities that *only they* can perform. Thus, the presiding Brethren have suggested that it is best to leave the sealing of couples and families to the "regularly ordained temple sealers."[2]

Notes

1. Boyd K. Packer, *The Holy Temple* (Salt Lake City, UT: Bookcraft, 1980), 68.
2. See Boyd K. Packer, *The Holy Temple* (Salt Lake City, UT: Bookcraft, 1980), 60–61.

69

Why can't family and friends who are not Latter-day Saints or are not endowed attend a temple sealing?

President Gordon B. Hinckley (1910–2008), fifteenth President of the Church, taught, "Each of our temples has on its face the statement, 'Holiness to the Lord,' to which I should like to add the injunction, 'Keep His house holy!'"[1] Those of us who have entered the temple and have made sacred covenants have an obligation to ensure that the house of the Lord is kept holy.

By this, I certainly *do not* wish to be understood as saying that non–Latter-day Saints or members of the Church who have yet to receive their endowment are somehow less holy than temple-going members of the Church. Rather, what I wish to imply is this: in order for you or I to qualify to enter one of the Lord's sacred temples, we must attest before two authorized witnesses that we are keeping all of the standards of the Church, that we are living the covenants we have made, and that we are worthy to be granted admittance to one of the most sacred sites on the face of the planet. The interview in which we attest to our worthiness takes time, and it surveys our beliefs, our faithfulness, and our activity in the Church, in addition to our commitment to live the standards *the Lord has set* for entrance into His house (see Question #12). There are many members of the Church who have chosen to *not* qualify for a temple recommend; thus, the Church is not discriminating against those not of our faith. The rule, policy, or commandment limiting who can enter a dedicated temple is based on the Lord's injunction that we only allow into His temples those who have made, or are about to make, certain higher covenants. A non–Latter-day Saint has not made these covenants and is not yet willing to. A temple-endowed Latter-day Saint who once qualified for a recommend but does not qualify for one now is apparently not currently keeping those higher covenants. In addition, a young member of the family who is not yet old enough to receive his or her endowment is most likely not mature enough to enter into such sacred higher covenants.[2] It is for this reason that certain people are excluded from watching a temple sealing.

While a bishop cannot interview a non–Latter-day Saint for a temple recommend, even if such were possible, the nonmember could not answer truthfully that they believe in *all* of the doctrine of the Church and keep *all* of the commandments—including tithing, the Word of Wisdom, attending *all* of their Latter-day Saint church meetings, and so on. If they could answer such questions, as is necessary to qualify for a temple recommend, they would most likely have joined the Church already. Moreover, a member of the Church who does not have a current temple recommend could certainly get one, if he or she so chooses, by living his or her life in harmony with his or her covenants and the Lord's commandments.

Of course, it is God's will that *all* of His children enter the temple to make and keep sacred covenants. However, the Lord knows that if those who have not made such covenants—or who are not committed to such covenants—are allowed to enter, the temple experience is at risk of becoming less sacred and less set apart from the world. If the doors of the temples were opened to all who wished to view or participate in an ordinance, in addition to the non-LDS family and friends who would like to attend, many of the Church's enemies would begin to fill the Lord's house, seek to disrupt the ceremonies therein, and would mock (there and in the press) the holy things we do in the temple. Thus, even if the Lord would allow it—which He has not—it would be impossible for bishops and stake presidents to determine which non-members would reverence what we do in our temples and which would mock and disrupt the sacred ceremonies (Matthew 7:6; 3 Nephi 14:6; D&C 41:6). Thus, only those who have made the higher covenants of the endowment and are keeping them are allowed to observe the sealing and endowment ceremonies.

I know firsthand the challenge this poses. I am a convert to The Church of Jesus Christ of Latter-day Saints and, when I was sealed to my spouse, I was not able to have *any* of my family in attendance at my sealing. For parents who have waited their entire lives to see a son or daughter married, this can be a heartbreaking thing. However, as President Boyd K. Packer (1924–2015), former President of the Quorum of the Twelve Apostles, has observed, "Prayerful and careful planning in most cases can make the problem transform itself into an opportunity that ultimately will bring the family closer together than it previously had been."[3] Here are a few suggestions that can help with this difficult challenge.[4]

- ◆ Talk about the temple and about temple marriage with those who would not be able to attend your sealing *well before* you are engaged. That will help them to anticipate the challenge and be less shocked by your decision to be married in the temple.

- ◆ Involve your non–Latter-day Saint or less-active family members in as much of the wedding and reception preparations as possible. Ask for their advice and, where possible, take it. Invite them to take certain assignments that will help them to feel they are making important contributions to the wedding and reception preparations.

- ◆ Look for opportunities to give your parents recognition, respect, and appreciation. You can do this at the wedding reception, but you may also want to explain your situation to the temple sealer and, if your parents are waiting at the temple, have him meet them in the foyer and share his thoughts about you and your spouse—and about what remarkable parents they must be to have raised such a child.

- ◆ You may want to write a letter or email to your family about how you feel about temple marriage. That will give them a chance to think about what this means to you without having to immediately respond.

- ◆ Perhaps take the family members who will not be able to be in attendance to a visitors' center *in advance of* the wedding day, and have a special tour that focuses on eternal marriage. Then take them to the temple grounds and even into the foyer of the temple so that they can feel the spirit of the temple and also feel familiar with the doctrine and the location.

♦ Tell them as much as would be appropriate about what will be happening during the sealing (see Question #63). One author suggested telling them, "In the temple, brides and grooms kneel at altars and clasp hands as a sealer ratifies their marriage with God's own binding seal."[5]

♦ Take time to speak with them shortly *before* the ceremony and, if possible, make them the first ones you go to *after* you exit the temple. This will help them to feel that they are the most important persons in your life and that you are grateful they are there with you to support you on this important day.

♦ Perhaps plan a small family gathering after the sealing but before the reception. At that, the bride and groom can express love for each other, though it would traditionally *not* be appropriate to exchange wedding vows at the gathering. You could reserve the exchanging of rings for that get-together rather than exchanging them in the temple, and perhaps you might mention how the rings represent the eternal nature of the marriage covenant. You may even wish to have a couple of hymns and prayers and a few words by the bishop regarding our beliefs about temple marriage and the eternal nature of families. All of this may help those not in attendance at the actual sealing to feel a sense of being part of this special day.

♦ If your family members who cannot attend the sealing will be waiting outside or in the temple's foyer, have an endowed member of the Church stay with them and talk with them about the doctrine of eternal families and about temple sealings. He or she could answer any questions that they might have.

♦ In order to help them feel less excluded, perhaps follow the example of this couple, whose family are not members of the Church:

> When my husband and I were planning our temple wedding, we did not feel right about inviting a large number of people to attend the sealing when both of our immediate families would be waiting outside. When our wedding day came, my husband and I went

to the temple to be sealed with only a few others in attendance. We felt blessed that it was simple and sweet and that our families did not feel so excluded.[6]

♦ Fast, pray, and put the names of those who will not be able to attend the sealing on the prayer roll of the temple. This will invite the Spirit to soften their hearts and help to bring a spirit of understanding and peace to their hearts and minds.

Notes

1. Gordon B. Hinckley, "Keeping the Temple Holy," in *Conference Report*, Apr. 1990, 69; or Ensign, May 1990, 50 & 52.
2. See Boyd K. Packer, *The Holy Temple* (Salt Lake City, UT: Bookcraft, 1980), 26–28.
3. Boyd K. Packer, *The Holy Temple* (Salt Lake City, UT: Bookcraft, 1980), 67.
4. Several of these suggestions are drawn from "Questions and Answers," in *Ensign*, February 2005, 32–35.
5. Adam S. Miller, *Letters to a Young Mormon*, second edition (Salt Lake City, UT: Deseret Book and the Maxwell Institute, 2007), 87. See also Elder Matthew Cowley, in *Conference Report*, October 1952, 27.
6. "Questions and Answers," in *Ensign*, February 2005, 35.

70

Do people getting sealed exchange wedding rings as part of the sealing ceremony?

While it is not part of the sealing ceremony, once the bride and groom are sealed—if they so desire—they may step away from the temple altar and exchange rings.[1] Some couples prefer to exchange their rings in the temple sealing room, and some prefer to do a ring exchange as part of their wedding reception. It is up to the bride and groom to decide what they prefer to do. If they decide to exchange rings in a location other than the sealing room, according to Church policy, that exchange should not be done elsewhere in the temple or on temple grounds. In addition, if they choose to exchange their rings at their reception, the exchange should not in any way appear to replicate any part of the temple sealing ceremony and should be done in a dignified manner that does not include the exchanging of vows.

Note

1. See Boyd K. Packer, *The Holy Temple* (Salt Lake City, UT: Bookcraft, 1980), 68.

What to Do Once
You've Received Your
Temple Ordinances

71

What if I didn't have an enjoyable experience the first time I attended the temple and don't really want to go back? What should I do?

When I was in college, I enrolled in a foreign language course. On the first day of class, about twenty-five of us were seated in the classroom, anxious to meet our new professor and to learn this ancient foreign language. The professor entered the room and, for the first twenty minutes or so, didn't speak a word of English to us. Instead, he tried to communicate with us using *only* the ancient language we had come to learn—but which none of us yet knew. The first twenty minutes of class were a total bust! Most of us did not have a very positive experience that first day. Everything was foreign. Nothing made sense. We learned nothing. Several of the students dropped the course, as they felt they didn't want to come back after that first difficult and unfamiliar experience. For some, this is how their first encounter with the temple endowment goes.

While I hope it is not a common occurrence, I suppose there may be a number of reasons why someone might not have a good experience the first time he or she participates in an endowment ceremony. Knowing that there occasionally are those who unfortunately do struggle with this, President David O. McKay (1873–1970), ninth President of the Church, explained:

> I have met . . . young people who have been disappointed after they have gone through the House of the Lord . . . Some of them have . . . expressed heart-felt sorrow that they did not see and

178

hear and feel what they had hoped to see and hear and feel. . . . I have come to the conclusion that in nearly every case . . . he or she has failed to comprehend the significance of the message that is given in the temple.[1]

President McKay's point is this: if you did not have a good experience the first time you participated in an endowment ceremony, perhaps that was because you didn't understand the meaning of what you were participating in. Anytime we encounter something new, we run the risk of not understanding it and, thus, not enjoying it. Such was the case with my foreign language class, and such can be the case with your temple experience.

So what should someone who did not have a great experience their first time through the temple do? Rather than not going back, I would suggest that the person who is struggling to enjoy the temple set out to really understand the endowment and its symbols, covenants, and doctrine. While I didn't enjoy my first day in our foreign language class, I went back, worked hard, and began to grasp the language. Consequently, I also began to *love* the language. Had I not returned to the class after my first frustrating experience, I would have missed out on an important part of my education. If you too decide to not return because your first encounter with the temple felt like a class in some ancient foreign language, you'll miss a very important and powerful part of your spiritual education.

No one expects to fully grasp the books of Isaiah or Revelation the first time they read them. We know we really have to pay a price for those books to not seem foreign and confusing to us. However, if one pays the price, one will begin to see marvelous things in those sacred texts. The same is true of the temple. If you'll set out to study it and understand it, God will turn that first challenging experience into something positive and fulfilling. (In Question #73, I have suggested some resources that will help you, once you have received your endowment, to better understand and appreciate what you experienced in the temple.)

Note

1. David O. McKay, "An Address on the Temple Ceremony," given to missionaries at the Salt Lake Temple Annex, Thursday, September 25, 1941. Harold B. Lee Library, Special Collections, Brigham Young University, 1.

{*72*}

How important is it that I understand what goes on in the various ordinances of the temple?

I suppose this question can be answered with another question: Do you care what God is trying to say to you through the ordinances of the temple? If you do, then the answer to "how important it is to understand what goes on in the temple?" is *VERY!*

Our goal is not simply to go to the temple to make covenants. Rather, the goal is to receive those sacred covenants, enter into them fully committed to living them, seek to understand all that they mean for our lives, and gain an understanding of the doctrinal teachings imbedded in the ceremonies in which those covenants are given. One doesn't, for example, go to the store to purchase a piece of fruit. Rather, one goes to get the fruit so that he or she can eat it, savor its wonderful taste, and be nourished by it. In attending the temple, if we want to experience the ordinances as delicious to our souls, and if we want to be nourished by them, then we have to really dig in and consume the whole package. We need to understand, as much as we are able, the various things God is saying to us, in addition to the covenants we make therein.

In response to the question "Are we expected to understand the Book of Revelation?" Elder Bruce R. McConkie (1915–1985), a member of the Quorum of the Twelve Apostles, wrote: "Certainly. Why else did the Lord reveal it? . . . The Lord expects us to seek wisdom, to ponder his revealed truths, and to gain a knowledge of them by the power of his Spirit. Otherwise he would not have revealed them unto us."[1] Just as we would need to pay a price in order to understand the book of Revelation, none of us will fully understand what God is trying to say to us in the temple without pondering, praying about, and researching what we are taught there. And to not do so—to take the approach that *if the Lord wants me to understand it, He'll just have to tell me what it all means*—is frankly lazy and undeserving of the tremendous insights that await those who are willing to pay a price to know and understand. President David O. McKay (1873–1970), ninth President of the Church, said that after receiving his endowment he went to the temple over and over again to study what was done and taught therein—and we should too![2]

I had been attending the temple for several years before getting married. I felt like I got the basic message of the various ordinances, and I didn't think there was much more to know or learn. I felt a bit bored each time I went, as there wasn't really anything new . . . or so I supposed. Shortly after we were married, my wife began to push a bit, saying we needed to get to the temple more often. I went, but with a lack of enthusiasm, as I didn't think it was terribly worth my time. At some point it struck me: *there must be more to this than I'm seeing.* I decided that, owing to all of the symbolism in the temple, perhaps the face-value meaning wasn't the *real* or *primary* meaning of the ordinances. I determined to throw myself into a serious study of the ordinances, covenants, and symbols of the house of the Lord. Before long, my study of the temple became exciting to me—and important, much like studying my scriptures. I began to see things I had never noticed before. I began to have more spiritual experiences in the temple. I began to see meaning and application beyond anything I could have imagined in those early years. The temple and its ordinances began to be "delicious" to me (Alma 32:28), and I'm convinced that they can be to you too—*if* you will pay the price to *really* study and understand what the Lord is trying to say to *you* in His holy house.

Notes

1. Bruce R. McConkie, "Understanding the Book of Revelation," in *Ensign*, September 1975, 87.
2. See Gregory A. Prince and William Robert Wright, *David O. McKay and the Rise of Modern Mormonism* (Salt Lake City, UT: University of Utah Press, 2001), 278.

73

What resources are there that will help me to better understand what I experienced in the temple?

The most important resource you have for understanding what the temple and its ordinances mean for you at this stage of your life would be the Spirit. As President Dallin H. Oaks once noted, "The ultimate knowledge comes by revelation."[1] As you are attentive, prayerful, and contemplative, the Holy Ghost will bring to your attention certain details from the various ordinances of the temple. Things will strike you in ways they never did before, and you will find that you are learning *through the Spirit* what various covenants and symbols mean.[2]

Other valuable resources for understanding the temple are the holy scriptures. Much of what we are taught in the temple is found in the standard works of the Church. For example, each time we participate in an endowment session, we view a reenactment of the stories of the Creation and the Fall. If one spends time examining the several accounts of these two stories in scripture (Genesis 1–3, Moses 2–4, Abraham 4–5), one is likely to learn "by study and also by faith" (D&C 88:118) more about what God is trying to teach in the endowment. The scriptures are a wonderful source for learning about the ordinances of the temple and also the doctrine that underlies why we do what we do in the house of the Lord.

The teachings of modern-day prophets and apostles can also illuminate for us what is meant by the covenants and ordinances of the temple. For example, various prophets of this dispensation have discussed the specific covenants we make in the temple and what their implications for our lives are. Others have spoken of some of the symbolism of the temple. Many have taught about the doctrine of the temple. As we spend time listening to their words and studying their talks, many of our questions about the temple will be answered.

Attending the temple frequently is also very helpful in getting a better understanding of what the Lord is trying to teach you through those sacred ordinances. If you'll go, and go frequently, you'll find that the teachings and covenants will begin to find place in your mind and heart. That will enable you to ponder them and their meaning when you're not in the temple; but it will also enable the Spirit to speak to you through those teachings and covenants—specifically because you will have begun to understand what they mean, and that understanding will facilitate personal revelation.

Of course, the *one* place we can freely talk about what goes on in the temple is *in the temple*, specifically in the celestial room. Thus, as questions arise, you may wish to attend the temple with someone you know and trust, and spend a little time with that person in the celestial room reverently discussing the thoughts, impressions, and questions you have. If some questions linger, you can make an appointment to speak with a member of the temple presidency.[3] However, remember that you can *and should* seek personal revelation regarding what you've experienced in the house of the Lord and how it applies to your life.

Finally, there are a number of Latter-day Saint authors and scholars who have written about the temple. Their books and articles can be a treasure trove of information in helping faithful Saints to expand their minds and broaden their visions about the meaning of those sacred ordinances. I myself have written a number of books on symbolism that directly touch on temple themes:

♦ *The Lost Language of Symbolism: An Essential Guide for Recognizing and Interpreting Symbols of the Gospel.* This encyclopedic work looks at various categories of symbolism, such as colors, clothing, body parts, the temple, names, directions, etc. It is a helpful reference for discovering what various things in the temple mean.

- *Sacred Symbols: Finding Meaning in Rites, Rituals, and Ordinances* (Deluxe Edition). This volume examines many different ancient rites, rituals, and ordinances that will look very familiar to temple-attending Latter-day Saints (starting with baptism and concluding with marrying at an altar holding hands). It explains some of their ancient meanings and also many modern applications of the symbols. It is a very useful primer for those trying to better understand the symbolism of the temple.
- *The Truth about Eden: Understanding the Fall and our Temple Experience.* This book is focused on the stories of the Creation and the Fall as depicted in the scriptures and the temple endowment. It examines why they are told and retold each time we attend an endowment session, and it helps the reader to better understand how those sacred stories apply in very important ways to their lives today.
- *Temple Reflections: Insights into the House of the Lord.* This volume is a collection of essays on various temple themes, including women in the temple, art and architecture in the temple, clothing, and much, much more. It draws the readers' attention to things they might not have noticed and also address things they might have long struggled with. It offers many unique and curious insights into what goes on in the house of the Lord.

There are many other texts and numerous other authors who have written helpful things regarding the temple and its ordinances. If Latter-day Saints are willing to pay a price, God will guide them (through the Holy Spirit) to the answers to their questions, and their temple worship will be rich and rewarding.

Notes

1. Dallin H. Oaks, "Scripture Reading and Revelation," in *Ensign*, January 1995, 7.
2. Ed J. Pinegar, *The Temple: Gaining Knowledge and Power in the House of the Lord* (American Fork, UT: Covenant Communications, 2014), 65.
3. Gordon B. Hinckley, "Keeping the Temple Holy," in *Ensign*, May 1990, 52.

74

Why don't the prophets just tell us what all of the symbolism in the temple means?

Many years ago, a temple president told me that President Gordon B. Hinckley (1910–2008), the fifteenth President of the Church, had given him some counsel. President Hinckley's advice was for the temple president to instruct the ordinance workers at the temple to not explain to the patrons visiting the temple what the various symbols meant—even if the ordinance workers felt they knew the meaning. President Hinckley's reasoning was simple: if you wrestle with the Spirit to gain revelation on the meaning and application of something that goes on in—or is taught in—the temple, you both learn the meaning and have a spiritual experience in the process. "If we just tell them the meaning," President Hinckley is purported to have said, "we rob them of those opportunities for personal revelation and the associated spiritual experiences."

This temple president then informed me that President Hinckley also expressed concern that ordinance workers might limit the meaning of the ordinances and symbols if they dogmatically explain to patrons what *they think* something means. President Hinckley apparently felt that the various symbols of the temple would have different meanings to different people at different times in their lives. For the General Authorities (or a given ordinance worker) to say something specifically means this or that runs the risk of shutting off other interpretations or applications that the Spirit might provide a patron. St. Hilary of Poitiers (AD 310–368) suggested, "Scripture consists not in what one reads, but in what one understands."[1] Similarly, President Dallin H. Oaks

(b. 1932), a member of the First Presidency, once stated, "scripture is not limited to what it meant when it was written but may also include what that scripture means to a reader today."[2] And so it is with the temple: what you understand—through the Spirit—about the symbolism of an ordinance or article of temple clothing may be more important for you than an interpretation someone else might offer you. Thus, the General Authorities are very careful to not dogmatically declare that the symbols of the temple mean this or that. As you work to understand the meaning and application of all that we do in the house of the Lord, the Spirit will tell you what a given ordinance, symbol, piece of art or architecture, or article of clothing should mean for you *at this stage of your life and progression.* And what it might mean at one point is not necessarily what it will mean at another point.

I remind the reader of the oft-quoted statement in the *Latter-day Saint Bible Dictionary* regarding prayer. There it states, "Prayer is a form of work and is an appointed means for obtaining the highest of all blessings."[3] If we desire blessings, we must work for them. That applies as much to the temple as it does to prayer. If we wish to understand what things taught or done in the house of the Lord mean, we need to work for revelation from the Spirit. These things are not doled out cheaply. They are sacred, and we must pay a price for them. If we are willing to work, not only will the revelation and understanding come, but in the process we will have spiritual experiences that will help us to know that God is there and that temple work is right and true.

Notes

1. Hilary, *Ad Constantium Augustum* II, 9, cited in Hugh Nibley, *The World and the Prophets* (Provo, UT: Foundation for Ancient Research and Mormon Studies, 1987), 202.
2. Dallin H. Oaks, "Scripture Reading and Revelation," in *Ensign*, January 1995, 8.
3. *LDS Bible Dictionary* (Salt Lake City, UT: The Church of Jesus Christ of Latter-day Saints, 2013), 707, S.v., "Prayer."

75

How will participating in temple ordinances change my life?

Your temple experience will be as life changing as *you* allow it to be. Or, as President Boyd K. Packer (1924–2015), former President of the Quorum of the Twelve Apostles, put it, "What we gain *from* the temple will depend to a large degree on what we take *to* the temple in the way of humility and reverence and a desire to learn. If we are teachable we will be taught by the Spirit, in the temple."[1]

As we have already noted in this book, there isn't anything "magic" about entering the temple or making covenants within the walls of those sacred buildings. If you are baptized but don't keep the covenants associated with your baptism, in God's eyes it is as though you were never baptized. The same is true of being ordained to the priesthood, receiving your endowment, or being sealed for time and for all eternity. These covenants only have power—here and in the hereafter—*if* you keep the covenants associated with each of these sacred ordinances. D&C 132:7 warns us: "All covenants, contracts, bonds, obligations, oaths, vows, performances, connections, associations, or expectations, that are not made and entered into and sealed by the Holy Spirit of promise, . . . are of no efficacy, virtue, or force in and after the resurrection from the dead; for all contracts that are not made unto this end have an end when men are dead." Section 132 is saying, in effect, that if you *don't* keep the covenant associated with the ordinance, the ordinance will *not* be life changing for you. It may be salvation changing, but it won't be life-changing (in a positive way). So you need to be faithful to the things you promise when you are baptized, confirmed, ordained, endowed, or sealed. Then these covenants will have power *in*, and impact *on*, your life.

Also, your temple experience will be life changing *if* you pay a price to *really* understand your covenants and the symbolism in which those covenants are shrouded. If you choose to be lazy and not put any significant effort into thinking about or studying the ordinances, covenants, and symbolism of the temple, you will be limited in how much you get out of them, you will be limited in how protected you feel because of them, and you will be limited in how inspired you feel by them. God is trying to speak to you through the things that are said and done in the temple. You need to put as much effort into researching the temple as you might if you were trying to really understand the book of Revelation, the book of Ezekiel, the book of Isaiah, or any other book of sacred scripture. When you are in the temple, you should focus and think, contemplate and wonder. When you are out of the temple, you should read and search, study and pray about the temple and its meaning for your life. If you want the temple to be life changing, you need to change your life and your approach to temple worship.

Finally, your temple experience will be life changing if you go frequently. None of us would assume that we could renew our baptismal covenants without attending Church and partaking of the sacrament on a regular basis. However, many in the Church think that they can go to the temple once or twice a year and somehow have the covenants they made when they were endowed or sealed remain vibrant, alive, and active. If we want our temple covenants to have impact, we really need to attend the temple as often as our schedule allows. That means actually scheduling time to be in the temple regularly, rather than simply saying to yourself, "If I have time this week/month, I'll zip over to the temple for a session." (If you live too far from a temple to make this happen, then schedule some regular time to do genealogy, and then submit those names to the temple so that the work can be done on their behalf. Also, spend time studying about the temple. There are many resources that can help you to better understand what you're not able to regularly participate in because of how far you live from the temple.)

There are blessings that come from regularly attending the house of the Lord and blessings that are lost by not being in the temple with frequency. If you wish the temple to be impactful, then *let it* impact you. There are very few ways of spending your time that will have a more positive influence upon you, your marriage, your family, and your salvation than being in the house of the Lord on a very regular basis.

It has been said, "No work is more of a protection to this Church than temple work . . . No work is more spiritually refining. No work we do gives us more power . . . Our labors in the temple cover us with a shield and a protection, both individually and as a people."[2] I testify that the temple absolutely *can be* life changing, but *only you* get to decide if it is that for you!

Notes

1. Boyd K. Packer, *The Holy Temple* (Salt Lake City, UT: Bookcraft, 1980), 42.
2. Boyd K. Packer, *The Holy Temple* (Salt Lake City, UT: Bookcraft, 1980), 265.

About the Author

B rother Gaskill was reared near Independence, Missouri, where he converted to The Church of Jesus Christ of Latter-day Saints in November 1984. Prior to his conversion, he was a practicing Greek Orthodox. One year after his baptism, he served a full-time mission in England.

Professionally, Brother Gaskill taught seminary for four years in southeastern Idaho, after which he was an institute director at Stanford University and at UC Berkeley. He is currently a professor of Church history and doctrine at Brigham Young University, where his primary teaching focus is world religions and Christian history.

He is the author of numerous articles and books, including

* *Converted: True Mormon Conversion Stories from 15 Religions*
* *Know Your Religions, Volume 3: A Comparative Look at Mormonism and Jehovah's Witnesses*
* *Temple Reflections: Insights into the House of the Lord*
* *Catholic and Mormon: A Theological Conversion*
* *Miracles of the Book of Mormon: A Guide to the Symbolic Messages*
* *Miracles of the New Testament: A Guide to the Symbolic Messages*
* *Miracles of the Old Testament: A Guide to the Symbolic Messages*
* *Remember: Sacred Truths We Must Never Forget*
* *The Lost Teachings of Jesus on the Sacred Place of Women*
* *Love at Home: Insights from the Lives of Latter-day Prophets*
* *The Truth about Eden: Understanding the Fall and Our Temple Experience*
* *Odds Are You're Going to Be Exalted: Evidence that the Plan of Salvation Works!*
* *The Nativity: Rediscover the Most Important Birth in All History*
* *The Savior and the Serpent: Unlocking the Docrine of the Fall*
* *The Lost Language of Symbolism: An Essential Guide for Recognizing and Interpreting Symbols of the Gospel*
* *Our Savior's Love: Hope & Healing in Christ*
* *Sacred Symbols: Finding Meaning in Rites, Rituals, and Ordinances*
* *65 Questions and Answers about Patriarchal Blessings*

He and his wife, Lori, are the parents of five children and reside in Payson, Utah.

Scan to visit

alonzogaskill.wordpress.com